"Definitive hope for spouses feeling lost and broken due to sexual addiction. Meg Wilson understands the tragedy of addiction and the wisdom in rebuilding."

—J. R. MAHON
Pastor, XXXchurch.com

"*Hope After Betrayal* is a strong and sure lifeline that thousands of women will reach for in a drowning moment. Meg offers careful, clear direction and encouragement in each chapter while unveiling the truth about sexual addiction. The final chapter, written by Meg's husband, will change every woman's opinion on the topic. This valuable tool should be required reading for every wife and every mother of sons."

—ROBIN JONES GUNN
Best-selling author of *Take Flight!*, a Sisterchicks devotional

"*Hope After Betrayal* is honest, practical, and challenging. Best of all, it's faithful to God's Word. A woman betrayed by her husband will connect with this book because it offers the ring of truth and great hope for true healing. Meg clearly identifies with the feelings of the betrayed and doesn't minimize consequences. At the same time she challenges readers to look deep within at what God wants to accomplish in their own lives."

—RANDY ALCORN
Author of *Deception* and *Heaven*

"*Hope After Betrayal* addresses one of the greatest challenges marriages are facing in the twenty-first century—the devastating effects of sexual addiction. Through sharing her own personal experience, Meg gives godly wisdom and hope to women who find themselves walking down a path they never pictured themselves taking. Many will be blessed with the resources shared in this book and in knowing they are not alone in this battle."

—DIANE ROBERTS
Author of *Betrayed Heart* and *Accept No Substitute*

"Meg Wilson's *Hope After Betrayal* is an honest book that also encourages honesty from the reader. I love how Meg intertwined her own story with the story of three other women to detail how sexual addiction began in their husbands' lives, and how they have followed God through the process of healing and forgiveness. I applaud Meg for laying this out there with such care and hope!"

—CLAY CROSSE
Holy Homes Ministries
Singer/songwriter, author

Hope
After
Betrayal

Hope After Betrayal

Healing When Sexual Addiction Invades Your Marriage

Meg Wilson

Kregel
Publications

Hope After Betrayal: Healing When Sexual Addiction Invades Your Marriage

© 2007 by Meg Wilson

Published by Kregel Publications, a division of Kregel, Inc., P.O. Box 2607, Grand Rapids, MI 49501.

In the interests of privacy, in many cases names have been changed.

Unless otherwise indicated, Scripture quotations are from *The Message*. Copyright © 1993, 1994, 1995, 1996, 2000, 2001, 2002. Used by permission of NavPress Publishing Group. All rights reserved.

Scripture quotations marked NIV are from the *Holy Bible, New International Version®*. Copyright © 1973, 1978, 1984 by International Bible Society. Used by permission of Zondervan. All rights reserved.

Library of Congress Cataloging-in-Publication Data
Wilson, Meg
 Hope after betrayal : healing when sexual addiction invades your marriage / by Meg Wilson.
     p. cm.
  1. Sex addicts—Religious life. 2. Sex addiction—Religious aspects—Christianity. 3. Marriage—Religious aspects—Christianity. 4. Christian women—Religious life. I. Title.
BV4596.S42W56   2007
248.8'627—dc22   2007033058

ISBN 978-0-8254-3935-3

Printed in the United States of America

07 08 09 10 11 / 5 4 3 2 1

To
my Lord and Savior,
Jesus Christ.
Apart from Him
I can do nothing.

Contents

My Path

How does a woman pick her way through the darkness? How does she pick up the pieces? How does she cope after discovering her husband has engaged in sexual activities outside of their marriage? Since you're holding this book, I'm guessing you, or someone close to you, has recently had her life devastated by sexual betrayal. Or perhaps your wound from betrayal is an old one, made worse by a believer, pastor, or counselor who offered well-meaning but unhelpful direction.

More than six years ago, the path of my life was altered forever. I was a suburban wife with two daughters, two cars, two pets, and a firm grasp on the American dream. Central to all of this was a loving and successful husband who loved the Lord. I had it all! Oh, there were the typical run-of-the-mill challenges of parenting and finances. I simply glossed them over and pressed on.

The first tremor began with a call from a close family friend who had moved out of state. My husband and I listened as Mark explained he was stepping down as deacon of his church. Mark confessed his ongoing struggle with Internet pornography. Stunned and saddened, we knew this man's heart, and the news simply didn't make sense to us.

In the days that followed, I spent a lot of time on the phone with Amy, Mark's wife. I doubt if I was any help to her. It was clear she had crossed over into a dark land I knew nothing about. There was a new hardness to her words, which struck the surface of her idyllic appearance, cracking the high-gloss polish. Listening prepared me, though, in ways I couldn't realize at the time.

The thought that my husband, Dave, might also be struggling with the same problem didn't even cross my mind. I would have bet our every last cent on my husband's fidelity and honesty.

A couple of months later, the storm clouds rolled in. Prompted by Mark's confession, my husband admitted that he, too, was struggling with pornography. As a salesman, he traveled, and the in-room adult movies were a temptation to him. My husband's revelation sent me into that strange dark land. Everything that I thought I knew about my husband suddenly seemed like a lie. I was groping in the shadows, where it seemed truth was lost. As sad as I'd been for my friend Amy, her reality was now my reality. This was no longer simply *her* story—it was *my* life.

At least I knew the person I could turn to. Amy became my comfort and a valuable resource. She recommended many books. I read . . . and read . . . but absorbing was a challenge. Clinical definitions of this new term, "Sexual Addiction" (SA), didn't bring me much hope or comfort. I wanted to understand this new land, a place where I was lost in dark feelings.

Every page I read confirmed that SA was my husband's problem and not my fault. At the same time, my every body flaw confirmed it was my fault. The books assured me I was not alone in the way I felt, yet I never felt more abandoned. According to everything I read, the Lord was with me, but I couldn't see Him in the dark of hopelessness.

Then I found some footing; the old Meg took over. I began to deal with my shame and sadness as I had in the past, by dragging myself back into the world of delusion. I stuffed, denied, and prayed the problem away. After all, my husband was sorry. His library of books on recovering from SA grew, and he seemed to be spending more time reading the Bible.

I thanked God it was *only* pornography and for the amazing heal-ing of my husband. Life was back to normal.

An acute awareness grew in me, though, regarding the prevalence of SA in our society. Women experiencing the same pain were every-where. I came to understand their language and recognized the hints of their hidden shame. Seemingly innocuous statements like, "My husband and I aren't connected," or "My marriage is in crisis," were flashing lights to me. It didn't take long to realize how insidious this addiction is, particularly in the church. I wanted to help.

God began to bring more hurting women to me, and I shared with them my testimony of hope. Compelled by their pain and ex-perience, and my desire to make a difference, I saw the need for a support group. Women whose husbands struggle with sexual addic-tion need a place to heal. Our church already had a group for men. God connected me with Sharon, another wife whose husband was in recovery, and we decided to act.

I approached our pastor, Martin. He suggested attending an exist-ing class for wives of sex addicts at another church to see if we could incorporate their program. Pastor Martin's suggestion was a wise one. For twelve weeks, Sharon and I became students in their sup-port group. There, more than just learning took place. God poured additional truth and light into our lives. The Lord was building sup-ports under us for what was to come, though I didn't see it at the time. I was too busy thanking Him that my story wasn't as severe as some of the other women's in my group.

The following spring the first Healing Hearts group started at our church. Ten ladies showed up for the first meeting. Excited to see God provide the same rapid recovery in the lives of each woman, I looked forward to each meeting. It was a privilege to watch the light of hope spread along the paths of these women. As they stepped into their first golden beams and out of some lies, the healing process began.

A few weeks into our class, however, my marriage took another traumatic nosedive. It was a Tuesday morning in spring. That eve-ning I was scheduled to share my story of hope at Healing Hearts. When I got out of the shower, I noticed the message light on the phone was blinking. Pushing the button, I listened to the familiar sound of my husband's voice. I loved the fact that he called me every day, sometimes more often—far more often, in fact, than he once did when he was away. Since he'd been out of town the past week, I was glad to listen . . . until it became clear that this was not a routine "Just wanted to say hi, honey" call.

"It's me," said Dave's voice. "I'm on my way home. We have to talk . . . I'll be there by two . . . so please be home—alone. I'll explain in person. My boss has been very supportive."

My heart went into overdrive, pounding in my ears. Every nerve ending snapped to attention. There was an unfamiliar edge to his voice. Something was very wrong. Why was Dave coming home three days early? I knew from the last sentence that he hadn't lost his job. But I could tell this was not good news. My brain spun as I went over the last two days he was home. He'd seemed distracted and distant. I assumed it was the stress of travel.

I tried to get some chores done, but all I did was count the minutes until 2:00. When Dave's car pulled into our drive, I felt the urge to flee.

He walked in, holding a softcover notebook. It was curled in from the edges, from being rolled and unrolled. The expression on his face was like nothing I'd seen before. The pain that was reflected in his eyes was about to be mine. He spoke first.

"I'm home because of Carl . . . you know . . . my men's group leader. I called him last night . . . and I confessed my relapse a few days ago. The guilt was eating me alive." He went on, fiddling with the notebook as I sat frozen. "Carl told me to get home and confess to you before you shared our story tonight to the ladies in your group. I didn't sleep at all last night. I stayed up, writing a timeline of my sexual addiction."

Suddenly, nothing else existed except for the drumming of my husband's voice and the journal he was holding—the pages that were about to change my life indelibly.

I knew from Dave's first disclosure two years prior that his compulsion started when he was only eleven years old, when he found his father's pornographic material. Porn became a coping mechanism for his feelings of low self-worth. His addiction had progressed to its current state. This time, though, he included the parts of his story he'd left out before. Dave had not been completely honest in his first disclosure. For over seventeen years his being unfaithful had been inconceivable to me, and because he feared that I'd leave, he omitted important facts. Though his desire to be free and healed was sincere, his conscious exclusion of pertinent information had left just enough for the Enemy to get a handhold. Satan waited for the right moment, grabbed it, and dragged Dave even deeper into the addiction.

This time, my husband had hit bottom. He described how, after his last sexual encounter, he felt that God had turned His back on him. Loneliness had been his lifelong companion, but this feeling of being estranged from God was darker still. Dave sensed that he'd be dead if he didn't come clean. His desperation to be free of his addiction was so great that he was willing to lose our nineteen-year marriage. He confessed every betrayal over the course of our lives together.

As he referred to his notebook, determined now not to omit anything, life as I defined it vanished. Reality no longer existed. Dreams died and were buried out of reach. All that remained was one large, black hole with a huge question mark in the middle.

As he shared further details of his sexual addiction and continuing struggle, my heart was broken again, only deeper this time. Nothing I learned through reading all those SA books prepared me in that moment. Had the wound been physical instead of emotional, I might be dead.

The first time Dave confessed, he left out a nonphysical encounter with a woman. Even though there had been no touching, that omission stalled any chance of his being healed. This time he admitted that since his last confession he'd had physical contact with a woman. And this time I was unable to see straight or even remember any prior progress. The only thoughts I had were what a trusting fool I'd been, and that my husband had been unfaithful.

The pain grew unbearable. If one of the women in my group were to tell me that her husband had just made such a confession, what would I have said to her? I needed every tool and reinforcement God could supply, but I felt it was all out of reach. This hurt felt too big . . . too painful . . . too hopeless for any remedy.

Dazed at first, I didn't see God; I could barely breathe. I remember feeling nothing except my legs shaking beneath me. It was as if they were no longer a part of my body. I sensed the shivering, but was unable to control it. All I could do was sit and listen, and shudder under unthinkable images unfolding before me. My mind was numb, unable to register pain at that level—God's wonderful design called shock.

One thought did filter through to me, though: *Don't make any rash decisions.* I somehow recognized that I needed to wait until God spoke. I could only hope He was still there . . . hope He was real. Looking back, I realize, of course, God was there and had guided what I said, but in that moment I could see only fear, darkness, and complete hopelessness.

Dave and I were still talking when one of our daughters arrived home from school. Had it really been two hours since Dave had walked in the door with his notebook? It felt like two minutes.

Dave panicked. "What do you want me to do?" he murmured. "Should I go to a hotel?"

Amazingly void of emotion, I sensed God setting the guidelines for me. I heard myself speak in a normal tone, like I was listening to a stranger read a list. "You'll stay in the house until I'm sure what to do . . . and hear something . . . think of something. Just because you're here today doesn't mean you'll be here two days from now. We'll try to keep things as normal as possible for the girls. We'll sleep in the same room, but there will be no physical contact between us. We'll be like roommates, with neither of us in the room when the other is dressing or showering."

That's all I knew. Then my mind reengaged as a tidal wave of disbelief hit again. *How did we get here? Haven't I done all the right things? What a fool I was.*

Not wanting to face the women in our group that night, I called my trusted friend Sharon to cancel. She grieved for me but convinced me to go. Later, I called and backed out again. Finally, she said she'd pick me up and was on her way to get me. She knew I needed the support.

The group didn't get the story of hope I'd originally planned. Instead, they got their worst nightmare laid out before them. My head was down as I shared. When I finished, I looked up slowly, expecting to see their disappointment. Instead, I saw only tear-streaked, caring faces. I was humbled. They listened, cried with me, and offered their support. That night was difficult for all of us. Many had their own fresh wounds, but I needed to be there and share mine. The only comment I remember making was, "It stinks." I could see no hope at that point, but their understanding was salve for my hurting heart.

Had I stayed home, hiding and feeling ashamed, I may have found myself stuck there, because at home the battle raged in my mind. Like many Christian women, I wondered if there was just the right prayer to take away the pain, but I knew the injury was too severe to be sidestepped with a single prayer or Bible verse. Added to the betrayal was the disclosure of the lies. I felt like a failure as a Christian and a wife. What wrong turn had brought me to this place?

Dave and I spent the next day apart. I cleared my calendar except for an appointment with Donna, a friend. We were originally getting together to discuss her becoming my mentor. She had no idea what our first meeting would hold. Donna listened, though. Then she shared about an emotional affair her husband had many years ago. She understood the pain of betrayal.

She even went with me to my doctor while I was tested for sexually transmitted diseases (STDs). I'd never sounded the depths of shame until that moment. I could see my doctor didn't know what to say. She tried to be professional and compassionate, but she didn't want too much information. My shame had splashed onto her.

When I came out, Donna's loving expression enabled me to take the next step. She was a godsend—the right person at the right time. All the while I was crying out, "Why, God? Why? Why me?" But she listened and cried with me, never once condemning my husband. Not only did she not see him as a monster, her opinion of him didn't seem to be altered. She allowed me to see the first glimmer of hope.

If you see yourself in my pain, I empathize with you beyond words. Know that you are not alone. There's a growing community of women like you and me, most are just still hiding.

I understand how fortunate I was to have women who could share this nightmare with me. The majority of women, however, feel as if there's no one they can talk to. Whether or not you're sure of your husband's sexual addiction at this point, you have a loving heavenly Father standing by, ready to listen and help. He's already led you to find this resource. Keep reading and don't stay in the place of darkness. Determine to find the path to hope. I'll be honest; this is not an easy glide over a sunny slope. It's hard work.

Saying that my husband and I sailed right into healing would be a gross overstatement. We still had to live through and process all the emotions and the very real pain. I had to move from my initial shock and go through all of the stages of grief. Grabbing hold of God's truths, one at time, moved me inch by inch toward faith and health. I reached out first to books, looking for the one that would give me hope. I didn't find it right away.

Giving my pain, fears, and emotions to God started the healing process. Still, the steps weren't exactly clean or the results instantaneous. I cried out to Him often, because many pieces of my pain were harder to let go of than others. But as He ministered to my need every time I picked up His Word, our relationship deepened. I could have missed Him had I not been willing to step out in faith even when my feelings caused me to doubt God's existence.

All the theories that I knew about the character and attributes of God now became reality. Acknowledging, for instance, that I needed Him to be my strength and shield was an important turning point for me. For the first time, I spoke prayers without worrying about how they sounded. I didn't try to clean them up before speaking to Christ. I let Him have everything, because God already knew my pain. Verbalizing those deep hurts became an act of trust and worship. My first prayer was, in fact, not at all eloquent. The words were honest and went something like this: "Okay, God, I know You didn't plan this, but it doesn't take You by surprise, either. You can somehow use this for good even though I can't see how right now. All I know is it stinks. I'm choosing to trust You, knowing I need Your help because I can't do this alone."

Almost before I'd finished speaking the words, something was revealed to my spirit, like a veil had been lifted, and I knew I'd be okay. God began to personally minister to the broken places. The results were not magical; my circumstances didn't disappear. But the adjustment of my attitude—my determination just to let go and trust—was beginning to make the difference.

Evidence of God's work and His personal care for me came each morning as I opened my daily devotional. This long-established discipline took on new meaning day after day as each Scripture and reading seemed written just for me. On day one, a verse in Isaiah 54:5 said that my Maker is my Husband. Genesis 22:14 simply said that the Lord would provide.

And so His loving encouragement continued day by day. I felt God's intimate touch in a new and powerful way. Even though I understood He answers prayers, this intervention on His part was more. I had no doubt that God was addressing my specific needs with His loving words of truth. As walking through a trial with a friend grows the relationship, so my faith rose and soared, sheltered beneath the wings of His personal care.

ACKNOWLEDGMENTS

It may take a village to raise a child, but it took a small city to raise this book. I could not move ahead without acknowledging my fellow citizens who have been instrumental in this process. Foremost, after God, is my amazing husband who jokingly calls himself "my source material." You are so much more. You are a walking example of God's grace, mercy, and redemptive power. Thank you for daily doing the hardest work of your life—allowing God to take you through the refining fires. You are my beloved, the father of two amazing daughters, and my hero. We are all better for having faced and survived the darkness of sexual addiction.

Laurel and Sarah, seeing your pain was almost as hard as living my own, but watching you both grow in your own time and then blossom in the light of the truth made the work of healing worth the effort. It keeps me working still. God has blessed you both with wisdom beyond your years and beauty that shines from your insides to your outsides. I can't wait to see how God will use you both.

As I looked back over the last several years of healing and at the incredible network God sent me, I am humbled. He provided supporters, prayer warriors, teachers, mentors, and co-laborers. The Holy Spirit guided the process from the beginning. In the darkest moments He sent Willie to speak truth to my husband; and for me he sent Dawn, Linda, Susan, and the women of East Hills Church. He uplifted me with encouragers: Allison, Prabha, Deanna, Eric, Jim, Dena, Chris, Shelley, Sarah, Lynette, and Shelly. Then there were the many prayer warriors, such as Diann, Gaylen, LeNnae, Velynn, Nita, and Beth. To help with the writing process, he sent my dear PPCs— Jaynie and Robin—plus my CWG mentor, Julie. Then there were my editors of the heart—Raelene and Mesu. All the folks at Kregel really moved to get this book into your hands quickly. My wise counselors Kathy, Ross, Paul, and Matt did more than they know.

For all the women who have come through Healing Hearts, you honored me with every deep hurt you shared. You are a constant reminder of God's amazing (and oh-so-limitless) love and provision for His hurting children. There is nothing our God can't do or reclaim if we will simply trust Him. My hope, my certainty, is in Christ alone. Thanks don't seem like enough, so blessings, *many* blessings, on each of you dear ones for letting Him use you on my behalf. And now those blessings will be passed on to all those who read this book.

Walking Your Path

Hope After Betrayal is designed to help you walk along this path of darkness and pain and into a place of light and hope. No matter how long ago your injury occurred, this book is for you. Others, including me, have taken this journey and fought their battles along the way.

But there's good news—hope is real. Regardless of what your husband has done, or is doing, there's always hope for those who seek help. I've seen people do the messy work that results in the beauty of healing. I understand the joy of catching a glimmer of light where darkness once reigned. I've been to depths of pain unimaginable, only to find that God was deeper still. His peace and healing are within your grasp, too. You can be whole again. You can experience hope after betrayal. I can say emphatically, this is work worth doing.

But God's definition for *hope* is not the same as ours. We think of *hope* as a wish or dream of something that might happen. God's definition of *hope* is "promise." Like all of His promises, it is an absolute. Hope in Christ can be defined as complete confidence in a certainty. This hope includes our eternal future, which Christ provided for through His obedience to the Father when He went to the cross. His return is equally assured. Our security in the midst of insecure circumstances can be found only in Christ and His never-failing promises to us. He is the Hope After Betrayal.

The best way to recognize God's direction is to look for Him in His love letter to us. That is why each chapter ends with "Path Lights"—specific Bible verses that apply to the topic of the chapter. Some of these Scriptures will be new to you, others you may already know. In addition to helping us recognize God's direction, I've included these verses because once we learn about God's character, then we will recognize His qualities in other people.

Because this book takes you on a journey of self-exploration, you are asked to keep a journal (please see appendix A for further direction). After the "Path Lights" are some questions and/or suggestions to give you a place to jump off in your writing. My only request is that you come to God with an open heart and put the greatest weight on God's Word and not mine.

But be warned; as you read, you may find some truths in these pages that you'd rather avoid. Every fiber of your being will cry out against the change needed to move forward. Read those parts over and over, though. Use your journal to write about what you're feeling, and don't move on until you're willing to apply that truth completely. Work through every word until the direction is clear for your next step.

There might be times you find yourself getting mad or wanting to balk. These feelings are okay. Tell God; He will listen. Wrestle with these new concepts through prayer and through your journaling or some other healthy outlet for expression. Process your thoughts no matter how raw. Don't bother to clean up the words for God. He has already seen your whole heart, and He still loves you completely.

Whether you're new at turning to God or have been a follower of Christ for many years, expect Him to reveal Himself as you read through these pages. He has not abandoned you. He is, in fact, calling you by name. You'll discover that our heavenly Father is more than able to guide you, and He wants you to know that He has much to teach you through your pain. The words He has placed in the Bible are His words of love to you, written with you in mind. So listen to His truths, even those that are costly and painful. God wants to work in you and through you without regard to what your husband does or does not do. Decide whom you will follow, whose voice you will listen to, and whom you will serve every day.

Path Lights

God's a safe-house for the battered,
  a sanctuary during bad times.
The moment you arrive, you relax;
  you're never sorry you knocked.
(Ps. 9:9–10)

For your Maker is your bridegroom,
  his name, GOD-of-the-Angel-Armies!
Your Redeemer is The Holy of Israel,
  known as God of the whole earth.
You were like an abandoned wife, devastated with grief,
  and GOD welcomed you back.
(Isa. 54:5–6)

We can be so sure that every detail in our lives of love for God is worked into something good. (Rom. 8:28)

Scripture reassures us, "No one who trusts God like this—heart and soul—will ever regret it." It's exactly the same no matter what a person's religious background may be: the same God for all of us, acting the same incredibly generous way to everyone who calls out for help. "Everyone who calls, 'Help, God!' gets help." (Rom. 10:11–13)

Journaling

Begin to absorb the above Scripture truths. Make them a guide. Look at, underline, and meditate on each one. Each time you open the Bible to reflect on the "Path Lights," expect God to show you healing truths. With the guiding light of truth, travelers are less likely to get lost or wander off the path and into dangerous territory. I understand how strong the feelings of despair and loneliness can be. See Jesus holding out His hands in love, and let the light of truth strengthen your faith. After all, Christ knows full well the pain of betrayal.

Look to Him as you journal, writing about your thoughts and feelings. Begin to formulate that first prayer of faith. Don't clean up your thoughts. Cry out to Him. Let His heart of love draw you into the safety and security of His presence. Let the truth of His power, love, and care for you begin to light the way to a brighter future.

CHAPTER 1

Blackout

Brutal Betrayal

Betrayal by the one I love left me in utter darkness. Suddenly I felt completely alone, or as if loneliness had taken me hostage. If this has happened to you, the first thing I want you to know is you are not alone. The very fact that you're holding this book means that others are out there, unseen. They are in your church, neighborhood, and circle of friends. Some don't yet know the truth, many are still in hiding. That feeling of being isolated in the darkness, though powerful, is based on a lie. At this moment there may be no one in the flesh you feel you can talk to, but Jesus stands ready to listen.

Over the past few years I've heard many heartbreaking stories from wives who have learned about their husband's secret sexual lives. This discovery, or its disclosure, is what I refer to as *blackout*. It's like sitting in a friendly, familiar room and suddenly having all the lights go out. The familiar surroundings take an unfamiliar form. Well-known objects become obstacles that trip us up. Fear shrouds us as we grope in the dark, searching for something to orient ourselves by.

Some would say the above descriptions are overstated. You may have family or friends who say that you're overreacting. After all, looking at pornography is "harmless" adult entertainment.

Fantasy doesn't harm anyone. Such opinions, though, are made out of ignorance and denial. Sexual addiction typically begins with the habitual use of porn combined with masturbation. This self-gratification conditions men to experience sex in isolation, moving them into what I call "the world of me." I've experienced firsthand the devastation a wife feels when she realizes the most intimate area of her heart has been betrayed. I've seen over and over the same pain in others, and only those who have been there truly understand it. But well-meaning onlookers, because they lack this understanding, often make comments that create additional wounds.

Blackout occurs in different ways and at different levels. Sometimes disclosure is quick, and it seems like someone flipped the off switch. More often, a bit of information starts a dimming process that, over time, ends in complete darkness. One reason for the slower progression is the way many men are discovered. Often, they're caught—a bill, note, or Web site gives them away—which leads to a partial confession. Even husbands who desire to come clean leave out critical information in the face of fear. Add to that an angry and hurting wife, and to many men, complete disclosure seems impossible.

The result for the wife is like candle flames being snuffed out one at a time, as he discloses or she discovers more and more information. But, in a diabolic twist of irony, a partial confession turns out to be worse than none at all. Husbands must confess everything in order for real healing to begin. Lies of omission are still dishonest even if well intentioned. Anything left in the darkness leaves a noose the Enemy can tighten at the opportune moment. Inevitably the rest of the story comes out later, increasing the wife's pain and making blackout complete.

While confession—what and how much to disclose—will be addressed more later, for now I suggest you use great caution in demanding too much detail from your husband. Morbid curiosity has left many a woman with too many images that are difficult to erase. The best thing is to get only the general facts needed, not the gory details.

When my husband got tired of running from the truth—and from God—he finally confessed everything. I took advantage of his desire to be completely honest. Looking back, I realize I asked some questions that crossed over the line of what I needed to know. Plagued by images I didn't need, the war raged in my head every time those images came up. Thanks to the teaching in my husband's men's group, there were times I'd ask questions and he would say, "I'll answer that question, but are you sure you want me to?" This was a good check. Realizing I had all the information I needed, I stopped asking for unnecessary details.

You may cringe at this next statement: If your husband has come to you and confessed all, you will eventually come to see that as fortunate. I was one of the fortunate few—my husband *did* come to me, though at the time I couldn't see how anything good could come out of it. Eventually, though, I recognized my husband's coming completely clean was the first truly positive step even though the further disclosure caused more pain for me. It was God's way of giving me a fresh perspective, and it was the real beginning of healing. Dave's complete disclosure helped me to realize I wasn't the only one hurting. It began to sink in that God was showing me Dave's years of pain. He was a broken man and God had let him hit bottom.

My anger cooled. Dave wasn't having fun. On the contrary, he'd been living a double life and battling demons since he was eleven years old. In addition, with his full confession he had to be willing to accept all of the potential consequences, including losing his marriage. He realized nothing could be worse than remaining where he was—in spiritual bondage.

I've encountered many wives who've had to deal with this same heartache of sexual betrayal, and I've repeatedly witnessed that once the whole truth has been revealed, even by accident, healing can start—for the husband, or wife, or both. Most men want help out of their bondage but are too ashamed to ask. Many have cried out to God in agony asking Him to release them from it. Every man believes, however, that if others knew fully what he has done, they wouldn't forgive him. This lie keeps him in hiding and away from healing.

His being discovered, then, can be a husband's first step on the road to freedom. But just as important, his being discovered can be a catalyst for the wife to get help—if shame doesn't keep her in hiding. Yes, I hated what I'd learned from Dave, but finding and dealing with the truth, though painful, was still healthier than living a lie. Accepting this reality, though, takes time. Part of me wanted to go back, to live in blissful ignorance. There was, of course, no going back. I couldn't pretend that I didn't know.

The potential for positive change started in those moments when the darkness shut out any light. Growth wasn't recognizable at first, but the loss of trust, security, innocence, and so many hopes brought me face-to-face with my need for God. A false foundation of security and comfort had kept me at arm's length from God. I'd placed my trust in my husband and on my own resources. Oh sure, I understood that Christians aren't immune from trials and from sickness and from natural disasters. But I'd trusted that my practicing of spiritual disciplines—praying, daily devotionals, attending church—would somehow protect me from the really big personal catastrophes.

It was time now to reach out to Him, even though I felt He hadn't lived up to His part of the bargain. I needed to disconnect from my dependence on false foundations and mourn the loss of those dreams that would never become a reality. Illusions of a perfect husband, partner, or family dissipated. After the shock wore off, I was engulfed by a swirl of emotions—sadness, depression, hopelessness, anger. Satan, the Father of Lies, was hard at work, adding his words of despair. He works hardest when we are most vulnerable.

At times, listening for God's voice took a conscious force of my will. I had to keep making that decision for faith and total dependence on God. I kept wanting answers: Why is this happening to me? When will this pain go away? Will I ever see light at the end of this tunnel? Letting go of my desire for control and my need for answers was excruciating. This complete reliance on God was a new place for me. I'd kept so much of my life under my control—deciding what committee I'd sit on, what personal ministry I'd pursue, which organization I'd contribute to, what cause I'd volunteer for. God was only necessary for Sundays and those really big life decisions. The day-to-day operation had been mine.

Then all of those faulty supports crumbled. The severity of the situation helped me realize that this crisis was too big to carry on my own. I needed a God-sized hand to reach down and give me support. Letting go of my death grip over my own security and reaching out instead to God, allowing Him to do His work, was my only viable option.

Although my spirit was clouded in despair, making the choice to believe cleared my vision. I concentrated on the soft and loving voice of my Savior, and not the shrill screech of hopelessness trying to break through. You see, a spiritual war was raging in my head. As I began to pay attention to my inner thoughts and the feelings they provoked, this connection of thoughts and feelings helped identify when God, rather than Satan or me, was speaking. God's voice spoke loving words and never brought condemnation or despair—only light, hope, and healing. Even His discipline produced hope, because this new path I'd chosen to follow was clear, and the old mistakes of trusting my security to the wrong people and things were forgotten. I began to understand that darkness, depression, and despair were the product of lies—lies that you'll read about in later chapters. Those lies kept my eyes on me or on Dave instead of focused on God.

With Christ, my situation was never beyond help. Sometimes just telling Him, "Lord, I feel like this situation is beyond help," led me to see that I could keep putting one foot in front of the other. What's more, I've seen that He is available to all who are willing to surrender to Him. Regardless of how severe the betrayal, women who choose to let go of their need to control the outcome of that betrayal and place their complete trust in Christ are never disappointed.

This doesn't mean everything will be resolved in a neat package, tied with a pretty bow. I don't want to minimize the truth here. Even after I handed it all over to God, I still needed to sift through a great deal of pain. I still needed regular self-reminders: *Meg, stop the wondering and the why-ing. You've handed this over to God.* Nor is every marriage healed. It's also true, however, that even the most broken places in your heart and spirit can become resplendent with faith and time. Every woman I know who has wholeheartedly sought God has found Him.

Women who were not willing to let God have their hurts, who

hung onto them for whatever reasons, tended to become stuck in a sad place with their pain. Their deepest pitfall was their failure to trust God. Their refusal or unwillingness to believe they could let go of their pain, shame, unforgiveness, anger, or entitlement left them floundering in the dark.

Are you unsure about wanting, or being able, to let go? That's okay. Simply take a chance. Ask God to help with the uncertainty—you have nothing to lose. On my own I could never have figured out God's plan, the plan the chapters of this book lay out for you. I needed Him to show me the impossible. Not only does He love to intervene in hopeless situations, He loves to do so much more than we could ever have thought or asked.

After I recognized God's presence, His leading about how I should cope with my situation became clearer. Although putting my life back together again seemed impossible, I knew that miracles come only out of the seemingly impossible, and when they do, God alone gets all of the credit.

Still, though God is all we need, He often sends others to come alongside us on our path. So I'd like to introduce you to three ladies. Consider them your personal support group. Learn by watching their lives. Tammy, Stephanie, and Renee are based on the dozens of women I've worked with over the past few years. Their lives, a blending together of many lives, represent situations, comments, and decisions faced by real women who were lost in the darkness of betrayal. They share what disclosure or discovery was like for them.

❧

Tammy is young, soft-spoken, and easy to like. She tosses her sandy hair when she talks, and she asks a lot of questions.

> I've always loved my glasses—because they came with rose-colored lenses—until I got *the* call one rainy afternoon. My husband's voice sounded odd, strained, and thin. He needed me to get a sitter and then come down to the police station to bail him out of jail—for soliciting a prostitute!

The adrenaline shot through my body, and my heart started to pound, but something kept me from screaming over the phone the million questions that ran through my mind. Instead, I squeaked out, "I'll be there."

As soon as I hung up, I felt . . . just very afraid. All the time I was making arrangements for the kids, I kept moving and checking—checking the time, checking to make sure the burners on the stove were off, checking that the answering machine was working. I didn't want time to think, because I didn't want to admit what was happening. Could it be a mistake? Things hadn't been great in my marriage for a while, but those darned rose-colored glasses—they made me assume that things would just get better in time.

As Tammy and her husband sat in the car after the paperwork was done, she felt as though she were covered in black, sticky tar. Shame was mixed with unbearable fear and dread. Her husband wasted no time as he shared his ongoing struggles. She sat silently as he described years of pornography, strip clubs, and eventually prostitutes. She tried to wash some of the tar off with a steady stream of tears.

I felt like I was suffocating. With his every word, his load lightened but mine got heavier. He wanted me to say, right then, if I was going to leave him or kick him out of the house. But I was in shock! The only words that came out were, "I can't breathe." Then I realized what a divorce would mean. The life of a single parent flashed before me, along with his face on the front page of the newspaper. Divorce would be like admitting failure. I wanted to believe that we could work everything out, but I couldn't see how. I handed him the keys, took a cab home, and entered my new reality.

Stephanie is an attractive brunette, always put-together, and all business. One quiet Saturday, she was surfing on the computer. She was glad to finally have some time to look up a popular shopping site. As she logged on, she looked up at the toolbar and saw the icon titled *History.*

My brain seemed to be connecting the dots, as though someone was leading me out of the confusion. Thoughts, like neon signs, were directing me. A recent memory flashed through my head—a friend talking about checking history on her son's computer. My heart started pounding as I remembered an article I'd read that week regarding men and Internet pornography. Then I realized the enormous amount of time my husband was spending surfing the net. I remembered that whenever I broached the subject, he would get defensive and accuse me, only half joking, of keeping him under surveillance. Those confrontations always left me feeling like I was being irrationally jealous.

This time, though, before ever tapping the mouse, I knew what I'd find. Site after site spewed from the printer, giving dates and length of time spent in the filth. There was no doubt about what those sites were. The explicit and crude names made clear what the content was. Watching the pages print out was like watching black clouds roll in. So many emotions were closing in on me like a dense fog.

I had to do something with the growing tempest and the list. My rational side tried to give my husband the benefit of the doubt. But there was no mistaking what had been taking place on our computer late at night—even last night.

After the fog thinned, doubts and fears rained down. Did I have a right to look at the history? Should I check phone bills, too, and credit card statements, and his briefcase? The thoughts were spinning out of control until I fell into a soggy pile on the floor. I'm an educated person, and when it came to adult entertainment, I was tolerant and open-minded. That was before—before I found out that the adult was *my* husband.

Renee is a down-to-earth redhead. She discovered her husband's affair through a phone call from one of his coworkers. She reacted quickly, with vengeance and rage. She was a clap of thunder followed by bolts of lightning.

> I was so ticked at my husband, kicking him out came natural. I couldn't even look at him. How could I be so repulsed by the man I loved? All I could see was him with someone else while I was this trusting fool at home, without a clue.
>
> All the pieces suddenly fell into place. I'd suspected something. My gut, and little changes, told me he was hiding something. Lately, he'd become moody and didn't want to talk about it. He began to worry more about his looks and even joined a gym. When was the last time he'd talked to me about important stuff—about what was going on in his head, or who was bugging him at work, or where he'd really like to go on our next vacation? I knew something was wrong. I just figured I was the problem. What a fool I was!
>
> I hated him—but I also felt rage toward the other woman. Anger seemed to be the only emotion I could put a name to. I prayed that I'd never run into her, because if that day ever came, the result would *not* be pretty. Overnight I began to feel hard, ugly, old, and used.

Responses to the secret lives of husbands are as varied as the women who discover them. But these women also feel some things in common—the initial disbelief, shock, anger, even self-blame. I remember the stories of the women in the first support group I attended. As I listened, I remember thinking, *Most of their experiences seem far more severe than mine. After all, my husband came clean before his addiction had progressed past pornography.* Comparing my story to theirs and minimizing what my husband did found me thanking God it was "only pornography."

This kind of thinking, though, is something to be avoided.

Comparing your situation to Tammy's, or Stephanie's, or Renee's, or to any woman's is not the goal. Instead, look for commonalities and pray for God to speak to you through other voices. Whenever I hear a new story, there's always some detail or emotion I can relate to. The pain is always the same even though the details vary. Some women, like me, minimize their situations. Other women use their details to maximize their situations. They decide their circumstances are worse than others', and they become supervictims. Actually, the pain of betrayal is brutal in any form.

Use the common aspects of our stories to recognize yourself, then learn from those who have gone before. Shared pain draws us together. Every time a new group starts, the fresh batch of raw emotions is palpable. With the assurance of confidentiality, each person shares, fostering an open and safe environment. Picture yourself with Tammy, Stephanie, Renee, and me. We are your small group. We want you to know that you are not alone. You are safe, and we understand all the emotions you're feeling.

When the blackout of betrayal drapes your spirit, you have trouble finding anything recognizable in your world. We want you to see that flicker of light that says, "There is an end to this darkness." If you absorb nothing else from these chapters, know that God is not thwarted by what has happened. His plan for your life is secure. He didn't want this, but He can work through it—if you'll let Him. If you're not sure you believe in God, don't worry—He believes in you, and He brought you to this place. "Now faith is being sure of what we hope for and certain of what we do not see" (Heb. 11:1 NIV). Right now you may not have hope for your future, and you probably don't yet see anything good. But be sure and be certain of it anyway.

After the disclosure, it's hard to be certain of anything—except pain. It's difficult to remember to eat, or even breathe, let alone to think or to pray. Whenever the situation seems just too big, that's the best time to ask for divine intervention. Your first prayers may be more of a knee-jerk reaction than anything concrete—"God help me!" and that's okay. Women, especially those of us who have been raised in the church, often look for the right words—the magic prayer that will take away the pain. We jump right to the best parts of the truth: "God is the God of love and healing" and "God works everything out for good." Although true, this is not the *whole* truth. The Bible doesn't say that we get to avoid going through pain. I don't know of anyone who has figured a way around that one. But it does say that God will walk us through the pain while meeting our needs in the midst of the darkness. His first concern is for our relationship with Him, not our circumstances.

Some betrayed wives believe that, because they're in pain, God is absent or missing. It breaks my heart when women believe this lie. In reality, when we are in pain, we find God at a deeper level. When life is pleasant or even normal, our experience of God is often like dessert after we've eaten a satisfying meal—it's appreciated and savored, like a blessing. But when we're in a crisis, our experience of God is like bread when we're starving; the Bread of Life is the nourishment that keeps us alive. He is like water when we're dying of thirst; the Living Water is beyond value. When we've had the spiritual wind knocked out of us, Christ acts as our next breath. Seek Him in the pain; there is no greater comforter or counselor than Jesus Christ.

The next lie women often buy into is believing that they are somehow to blame for their husband's betrayal. Whether they conclude they should be more attractive, available, supportive, thinner, curvaceous, or less of a nag, the lie is the same—they think it's their fault. The Enemy feeds this lie with whatever our weakness is.

For me it was my secret belief that only really beautiful people find happiness. It sounds silly even to write it now, yet something deep within me believed that I wasn't woman enough.

When I was growing up, some of my family members placed too much emphasis on appearance and weight. No one actually criticized me, but I watched family members struggle for years with body issues and be critical of themselves and others. The message was clear as glass. Slender, attractive women have more value. Movies, commercials, media, and the school yard continually supported this belief. There was plenty of misinformation to reinforce the lie that attractiveness equals self-worth.

Having dozens of "beautiful" types come into our support group has really blown this lie out of the water. I'll never forget walking into that first support group. There were thirty to forty women—and they were all beautiful! There simply is no connection between a wife's attractiveness and her husband's sexual addiction. Those who think otherwise don't understand how the addiction works.

Sexual addiction is simply someone's using the natural drugs found in his or her brain chemistry to medicate emotional pain. It's not about sex. Let me say this again, because I know people have a hard time grasping this truth: Sexual addiction is not about sex; it's about escaping and avoiding pain.

Every story I've heard begins with how the addiction started when the man was young. On average, the young man's first sexual exposure occurred when he was between nine and fourteen years of age, with the earliest at age five. So most men are deep into the addiction long before any real relationship with the opposite sex begins.

Since boys at these young ages can't easily buy beer or illegal drugs, many discover a different way to dull their pain or cope. Through sexual arousal, all of their problems seem to disappear. When they look at or read sexually graphic material, endorphins and enkephalins are released in their brains, causing a high. These chemicals give the feeling of euphoria and a false sense of manliness. Addicts in their own minds are kings.

It's important to understand the basis and nature of this addiction, not as an excuse or justification, but as a point of reference. The facts simply do not support the belief that the wife is at fault; the husband came to her already dependent. Most men assumed it would end once they were married. Their feelings of love for their wives were sincere, so why would they need anything else to satisfy them? The sad truth is that the addiction already had taken control.

As you read other resources, you'll find these same facts. I needed to hear the same thing repeated several times before I finally *heard* it. In listening to or reading the stories of recovering sex addicts, I encountered the same things described over and over. The truth at last sunk in. My husband's addiction was not about me. I wasn't there when it started. I didn't do anything to cause it. And I could not change it.

Truth is a powerful healer.

My hope is that these pages give you a flicker of light, or perhaps a voice that whispers, "There is hope and a future. The present darkness will not last forever. Vision will be restored as you find God's light of truth and cast off the shroud of lies." To get there, though, is a process. And I won't minimize the time and hard work it takes.

What kind of work? A lot of it is spiritual work. Though it was not part of God's plan for people to become addicts and create pain for those who love them, He can use everything we give to Him to make us stronger and more faithful followers. As we learn to stay in the arena of truth, we change, and so does the world around us. We gain a measure of control over our responses, we learn who we are in Christ, and we face obstacles with more confidence. The world becomes less threatening and no longer defines us.

Take this opportunity to see if God really exists. Unlike man, God will never leave nor could He ever be unfaithful. Let Him hold you, heal your broken places, and guide your next step.

Don't be surprised, though, if you hear another voice—that of despair, which would love for you to believe you are alone. Don't believe it! You don't have to get stuck in the pain, nor should you be defined by it. God is with you right now, and He will bring others into your life as ministers and encouragers. I pray that this book is a part of His process as we move forward together along this path.

Here are the first few glimmers of light to help guide you. Say them and let them penetrate your dark place:

- There is pain.
- There is hope.
- It's not my fault.
- I am never alone.
- I can place my entire situation in God's hands.

Path Lights

Trust GOD from the bottom of your heart;
don't try to figure out everything on your own.

Listen for GOD's voice in everything you do, everywhere you go;
he's the one who will keep you on track.

(Prov. 3:5–6)

I'm absolutely convinced that nothing . . . absolutely *nothing*
can get between us and God's love because of the way that
Jesus our Master has embraced us. (Rom. 8:38–39)

There's far more to this life than trusting in Christ. There's
also suffering for him. And the suffering is as much a gift as
the trusting. (Phil. 1:29)

So let's do it—full of belief, confident that we're presentable
inside and out. Let's keep a firm grip on the promises that
keep us going. He always keeps his word. (Heb. 10:22–23)

Since God assured us, "I'll never let you down, never walk
off and leave you," we can boldly quote,

> God is there, ready to help;
> I'm fearless no matter what.
> Who or what can get to me?
> (Heb. 13:5–6)

Journaling

As you begin to journal your thoughts about what has happened,
write out your answers to the questions below. Be honest about all
the feelings and pain. If you doubt God even exists, write that down
and tell Him. Take all of the thoughts that are revolving in your
mind and put them on paper. When you're done, look them over
and see what stands out. Now place them all in the hands of God,
and see what He does.

1. What were your initial thoughts and feelings when you discovered, or your husband disclosed, his sexual addition?
2. Where do you feel God is in your situation right now?

CHAPTER 2

Shrouded

Waiting for Direction

Waiting for direction isn't easy. When the blackout of betrayal shrouded me, I sat there in the darkness, knowing I needed to respond. But how? My initial reaction was strong, as it is for most women. And it's usually based in fear, and stemming from varying degrees of pain and anger. We're afraid of the unknown—what happens next. Doubts about making the right choices leave us confused. Unable to decide which way to go, we instead move around in a swirl of emotions.

At the moment of blackout, we're angry at our spouses, at others involved, or at God. The anger then usually morphs into fear. That fear attaches itself to any number of preexisting issues like low self-esteem—"Is there something wrong with me?"—or lack of self-control—"How can I hurt him back?" All these emotions and issues can easily lead the betrayed spouse into rash actions that may cause even more damage to all parties concerned. The extent of ongoing damage seems to depend on our initial reaction, so the goal is to minimize the damage that occurs at the point of blackout.

On more than one occasion, I've been in a pitch-black garage, caught there after the automatic garage-door light went off. So I know how important it is to move slowly, searching my way until I can orient myself—"There's the lawnmower . . . next should be my daughter's bike . . . ah . . . here are the stair-steps into the house"—or until my eyes adjust, or I find a source of light.

After Dave's disclosure I was caught in a flurry of possible choices. I have to confess that, in the face of my pain, I was sorely tempted to give in to a knee-jerk reaction without giving any thought to the outcomes. Our tendency is to look for quick solutions in all the wrong places—in our emotions, from our friends, in solutions that worked in the past—rather than wait for the best choice to be revealed through careful searching. It takes time for our eyes to adjust to the darkness. Trusting only in what we think we know can easily cause more bumps and bangs. When I get caught in a dark garage, I have to consider the possibility that someone may have left the lawnmower in front of the stair-steps. In a spiritual blackout, we need to identify, recognize, and remove obstacles that can lead to further damage.

Complete surrender to God's direction is the only way we can thread our way along the dark path. But everything in us yells at us to gain control, to thrash around in the dark and find our own way out. That panic and thrashing is why it's so important to wait before we act. We need to put an emotional space after the blackout but before the rash choice. Emotionally moving away from the pain enables us to look at the situation with some objectivity. All of the energy spent in our emotional thrashing about needs to be put instead into listening for God's healing voice. Let Him lead the way even though you don't know where it goes. Wait and see what only He can do.

So how did I know if it was God or me who was in control? The best way is to wait for the Word of God, the input of the people of God (mature believers), and the Spirit of God to line up. When the response I was thinking of was confirmed by the Bible, by others whom I trusted, and by a feeling of peace about the decision, then I could move forward in confidence.

Another reason I needed to seek God's guidance is based on the nature of addiction. Because I'd been living with an addict, certain patterns had been established in Dave's and my relationship. These patterns will be discussed later, but the point is, God can use disclosure to be the catalyst for looking for, recognizing, and changing those patterns, and for ultimate healing. I needed to be willing to let God show me my own part in the unhealthiness. Although wives are in no way responsible for their husband's addiction, we always have our own issues to address. My challenge was to determine what had kept me in the dark for so long.

At first, I wanted to focus on what my husband had done. That's the safest and most common tendency for betrayed wives. Standing back on our perceived innocence and pointing a finger just feels *so* right. I spent a lot of time reminding God of all the ways I'd been a faithful and loving wife. God listened patiently and then gently revealed to me more of the truth.

I'd always known I was responsible for my reactions, responses, and relationship with Christ. I know that one day I'll stand before the Lord and give an account. No one else will stand with me. I can't blame my spouse for the choices I've made. Nor is anyone without sin, not one—not me. I knew this was true, but I wanted to apply a sliding scale to measure my "little" sins. So I asked God, "Why couldn't I have married a little sinner like me?" I was stuck there for a while. How could God have let me marry this man? Why hadn't his addiction come out years earlier? I was full of questions.

God listened.

Then He gently and lovingly showed me how things looked from His vantage point. *Sin* means, "To miss the mark," and it encompasses more than I might think. Not just the "biggies" like murder and adultery. A superior attitude, for example, is off the mark: "My sins are miniscule compared to my husband's." This belief prevented me from receiving all God wanted for me—such as becoming more Christlike—and hindered my healing process.

Another way I missed the mark was to lean on my own understanding, which is a vastly limited understanding. The right thing to do didn't always make sense to my limited way of thinking. The whole truth was that every time I decided not to follow Christ, I was disobedient—I was in sin.

God showed me that *all* sin separates me from Him and every sin has the same, inestimable price tag—the blood of His Son. Though my sin may not have the same consequences as other sins, it is just as costly to God. My responsibility begins and ends solely with my choices in the presence of the Almighty.

Let's get back to the three ladies in our small support group and listen in on their choices.

⚮

Tammy, coming face-to-face with reality after her husband's arrest, didn't know which way to turn. Even after her husband confessed everything, she knew she had to make some decisions, but she felt paralyzed. She couldn't see how God could redeem any part of her situation. She was no longer sure about who God was. How could He let this happen?

> After coming home from picking up my husband at the jail, I felt like the wind had been permanently knocked out of me. I wanted to go to bed and never wake up. I'm not sure I would've gotten up at all if it weren't for the kids. My one certainty was I didn't want to be near my husband. I asked him to sleep in the guest room. The only reason I didn't ask him to move out was the kids—and a thin bedraggled strand of hope.
>
> Waves of pain washed over me, and I felt powerless to avoid them. It took every ounce of will to put food into my mouth. My weight dropped, and I felt exhausted. The only thing that was easy was crying. I knew I had to do something—but what? I thought that maybe I should focus on all the good things my husband had done in the past. After all, he wasn't all bad. Maybe if I prayed harder, that would help. But I didn't feel like praying.
>
> There was always something to bring back another wave of pain. Pay to get the car out of impound. Get a lawyer. Go to court. An acquaintance of mine found out what had happened. Meet with the pastor. More questions. I was sure the communication lines to heaven had been shut down, and I

floundered. I thought that God must have abandoned me, yet I still wanted to hear His voice. Something told me to hold on.

❧

Stephanie had decided that, after she confronted her husband about his use of Internet pornography, she would stuff the pain and put all her energy into helping him move forward. She would attack this problem like any other—with education and logic. She thought her husband alone had a problem, but that she could help. She would stand by him no matter what, knowing God hates divorce.

When I showed the printout to my husband, his reaction caught me off guard. He turned on me, calling me a snoop— and worse. This was not how I'd imagined the discussion would go. Suddenly my problems were a lot bigger. Deciding the best thing to do was research, I bought all the books I could find on sexual addiction. I even made copies of key pages and left them in places where my husband would see them, hoping he'd be interested in reading them.

I took a critical look at my appearance, which prompted some changes. Surely some sexier clothes would help keep my husband's interest. I contemplated plastic surgery. I also made sure to be available sexually at all times. Every effort only made him more angry and withdrawn. I just need to find the right tactic . . .

❧

After the call from her husband's coworker, Renee's decisions were based more on instinct than on thought. She let her pain do the talking.

All I wanted was revenge. I didn't take time to think about what the consequences might be. After I discovered my husband's affair, I was so angry all I wanted to do was make him the bad guy. Everything I did was aimed at getting back at him. I thought that would make me feel better. I wanted to give him some of the pain he'd given me.

Then to get back at me, my husband served me with divorce papers. It all happened so fast! I'd never really wanted a divorce. I wanted to make a point, get revenge, and gain control—yes—but divorce? No!

Well, if that's what he wanted, then I'd get the best divorce lawyer in town and get the largest settlement in history. If he wanted a fight, I'd give it to him. I was sure that no judge would be on *his* side. He'd abandoned *me*, and I just knew that the court would make him pay.

Then a few days later, I walked into our local coffee shop and saw my husband with that woman. I had to leave. My rage was boiling like molten lava. I knew if I opened my mouth, nothing but red-hot hate would come out. I was surprised at how shaken I was by my thoughts, with imagining in detail what I wanted to do to her. How did I get to this place? How long would I have to live with this bitter taste in my mouth and this sick feeling in my gut?

⸎

The choice to let God do the work in rebuilding your marriage takes faith, and it takes a strength of will to keep making that choice over and over. The tendency to take things into our own hands comes much easier. Some women, like Tammy, seek self-protection, and fall into the role of a victim. Others, like Stephanie, try to understand, or somehow figure out, what happened. Trying to make sense of addiction, though, is futile, because addiction is insanity. A man giving up his loving wife to be with himself or some stranger makes no sense. Still other women, like Renee, act on impulse.

When we try to take control of our crises, we usually resort to unhealthy means. Women like Renee blow up; many like Tammy withdraw and put themselves in danger of imploding; some like

Stephanie rationalize. Minimizing and spiritualizing are other means of denial, which are discussed below. Blame is not as blatant a coping mechanism as explosive anger but is no less destructive. Any method, or any combination of methods, is only a form of denial to sidestep reality, and so is based in lies. Any method of avoidance only aggravates our problem and keeps us stumbling around in the darkness.

Tammy, for instance, went into a type of withdrawal as well as victimhood. Her denial also included minimizing to avoid having to deal with a trauma. She minimized by trying to water down her husband's poor choices with his past good ones. In truth, though, those actions were independent of each other; good choices don't cancel out bad ones.

The list of minimizing and rationalizing statements is a long one. Some are, "It could be worse," or "Compared to other men, he's not so bad," or "Nobody's perfect." Tammy then rationalized her choices as necessary to protect her children. The choices we make, however, must be based in truth. We'll talk more about children later, but for now it's enough to say that they should not be used to sidestep truth.

Another way to minimize, with a bit of rationalization thrown in, is to convince ourselves that pornography isn't that bad. Finding support for this position is easy, especially among casual observers. A lot of people feel pornography is harmless entertainment that doesn't hurt anyone. But these people aren't the wives of the habitual porn users—nor are they correct. They simply haven't seen firsthand the destruction that families suffer after addiction to pornography is disclosed. Nor does ignoring the connection between pornography and sex offenders change the factual and statistical link. Studies have shown that men who regularly view sexual images have less respect for women. These men become conditioned to objectify women and can become increasingly more violent toward them. Minimizing and rationalizing the use of pornography also includes making excuses for a husband's behavior: "After all, he's under a lot of stress and needs a release," or "At least he comes home to me."

Self-blame is one of the most subtle lies that our Enemy whispers in the darkness. Most of us betrayed wives have ended up trying to compete with "it," even when we weren't sure what "it" was. Some women even get caught up in the addiction, agreeing to view pornography with their husbands, telling themselves that their sex lives will improve. Most end up feeling used and cheap when it becomes clear that, for their husbands, the sex act is all about feeding a physical addiction and not at all about connecting with them at a heart level.

Spiritualizing is another subtle lie. We take a bit of truth about God and bend it to help us cope with the situation and avoid dealing with the pain. Tammy knew, for example, that God works all things together for good. Though the words are true, the way she interpreted them was not. God works through us and in us, not in spite of us. She was expecting God to just take care of everything while forgetting that she had a part to play. He does work all things together for good—but only all things that we surrender to His control. It's hard to release control and let Him guide the process, but He can't work without our obedience and trust. Saying the right prayer, knowing Scripture by heart, and loving the Lord doesn't mean we get to bypass pain. Jesus doesn't take pain away; He walks with us and carries us through it.

In Stephanie's case, she tried to take on her husband's healing by rationalizing. She thought that if she could only find the right article or logical approach, she could change him. She kept trying to find her own answer, not willing to see what God wanted to show her. When we try to work out of a crisis in our own way, it's inevitable that we'll make poor choices, even though God doesn't desire them. The One who knows everything won't take away our free will, but He will hold our hand and walk us through the trials that come as a result of wrong turns.

Blame as a coping mechanism isn't always as explosive as Renee's. Sometimes resentment smolders like magma beneath the earth's crust, and each humiliation remembered by the injured wife builds more pressure beneath the surface. Anyone—the husband, the other woman, well-meaning friends—who might walk near the heat gets burned. The searing is usually done through sarcasm, mean-spiritedness, even profanity that bubbles to the surface. The children, too, can get splattered with lava if they mention something about Dad or act out because of anxiety. Whether it explodes or smolders, blame is about turning the focus elsewhere.

Let me say a word right here about judging the sex addict. It only makes sense to look at certain behaviors, including our own, as good or bad choices. Any person who engages in extramarital sexual activities has made a bad choice. Saying so or thinking so is not being judgmental—it's noticing a fact. Taking it upon ourselves to "fix" someone else or to administer punishment *is* being judgmental. Each of us is responsible for working on our own thoughts and behaviors. This is, in fact, our life's labor, and we'll never be done with ourselves. Surely we aren't qualified to fix anyone else, so it's best to leave the judgments to God. He is the only one who is fully competent and fair.

Blame, then, is a deceptive tactic. While it feels right, a wife's focusing on her husband's behavior prevents her from looking at her own. Although we did nothing to cause our husband's addiction or affair, we are responsible for our reactions. And that's where we can begin.

Each of the methods talked about above is based on subtle lies, is a form of denial, and is a way of avoiding some or all of the facts. I've heard many reasons for using them, but never one based on complete truth. Using any of them only delays the need to face up to the painful reality of the situation, and they leave the wife feeling powerless and defeated.

Nothing works better than recognizing the lies and acknowledging the truth. Complete honesty is the only path for moving toward health. Returning to the path of healing from the detour of denial is only part of the solution. Just as necessary a way is found in introspection. This, too, can be dangerous territory because it often brings a flood of self-doubt or mistaken conclusions. In my case, introspection at first revealed only darkness and fear. Even though I was trying to trust God, a shroud of lies kept falling over me, and I couldn't sort through them all at once.

I told myself that my husband's addiction was not about me, but all the old lies I felt about myself kept surfacing. The voice of despair told me I couldn't measure up. I tried to make myself believe, while growing more critical of my looks, weight, and shortcomings. My imagination was torture. I wondered every day about the physical attributes of the women my husband had seen, and how I must pale in comparison. It drove me deeper into unhealthy patterns until I couldn't even begin to find the first rays of the light of truth.

At this point I must interject a warning. Wounded women are vulnerable to an affair. One bit of attention from the wrong man can be like water to a dry sponge. Our need for assurance is at an all-time high: "If another man is attracted to me, I must be okay." It doesn't take much effort to put a tattered self-esteem that was naively placed in a husband's hand and place it in the hands of another man. It needs rather to be in the hands of God—the only place we'll find our worth. Add to the vulnerability false justification—"I'm only doing what my husband did"—and suddenly we're detoured down another wrong road. Be careful not to trade in one wound for a whole bundle of them.

The godly, brotherly support from a Christian man can, though, be healing. Whether a counselor, pastor, or friend, this man must be mature enough to keep appropriate boundaries. If not, run the other way. In my case, the support came from a man who is a recovering sex addict (all addicts are recovering one day at a time, for the rest of their lives), and when I heard him confirm my husband's experience, it was healing for me. His words let in some light through the shroud of my many nagging doubts. He stated emphatically that images or even acting out could never compare to reality. Fantasy is about an escape and a false intimacy, leaving the person spiritually void. I'd read similar words, but hearing it from another man was powerful. The truth set me free from attempting to compete with fantasy and enabled me to let go of the lie that I was somehow at fault.

God used this man to show me how much I had to offer my husband. His false sexual reality could never compare to the soul-satisfying connection of real love, any more than a photo of a blanket can provide the same warmth as the real thing. I could offer the lasting beauty of love and commitment that goes deeper than anything that is solely physical. Companionship and support are the real cords that tie two people for life. Intimacy comes from this heart connection, and married sex is the physical expression of this emotional and spiritual closeness. Focusing on the external alone is incomplete; we can't use sex to work backward toward real intimacy. This lack of intimacy is what the world offers, and is hollow and distorted compared to the real love God intended for husbands and wives.

I made the mistake of placing much of my self-worth and happiness in my husband, and I expected him to make me feel valuable, desirable, and significant. He was my god. When my idol proved to have feet of clay, the discovery fed my self-doubts. Many cords of security, mistakenly attached to my husband, needed to be disconnected and plugged into the right source—the power of God.

How, though, could Christ make me whole and provide my significance? I had to trust Him. Forging that trust was not a simple process, but Christ was patiently waiting for me to put all of myself into His hands. I had expected my husband to fill a place he never could, because Christ alone, as the only One who fully knows my heart's desires, can completely meet my needs. The more strongly I grabbed hold of this truth, the stronger I could stand alone, and the less I was affected by my husband's choices.

Daily, Christ proved trustworthy. Regardless of my husband's decisions, safety was mine in Jesus. He really was all I needed. As God's light penetrated the dark pockets of my denial, one at a time, my vision improved. These glimmers lit my path, forever improving how I would see the picture of my life and my future.

- I am responsible for my reactions.
- I am responsible only for me.
- God is all I need.
- Nothing is too big for God.
- I can trust God with everything.
- God's love for me is not conditional.

Path Lights

Complain if you must, but don't lash out.
Keep your mouth shut, and let your heart do the talking.
Build your case before God and wait for his verdict.

> (Ps. 4:4–5)

> Quiet down before GOD,
> be prayerful before him.
> (Ps. 37:7)

The lips of a seductive woman are oh so sweet,
    her soft words are oh so smooth.
But it won't be long before she's gravel in your mouth,
    a pain in your gut, a wound in your heart.

> (Prov. 5:3–4)

It's easy to see a smudge on your neighbor's face and be oblivious to the ugly sneer on your own. Do you have the nerve to say, "Let me wash your face for you," when your own face is distorted by contempt? (Luke 6:41–42)

Do you think anyone is going to be able to drive a wedge between us and Christ's love for us? There is no way! Not trouble, not hard times, not hatred, not hunger, not homelessness, not bullying threats, not backstabbing, not even the worst sins listed in Scripture. (Rom. 8:35)

Journaling

This week, journal your thoughts about marriage and God's plan for marriage. Process some of the expectations you brought with you to your marriage: What were they? How did they compare to reality? How do you feel about them now? Mourn the loss of the Cinderella story and the perfect family image. Now let God draw another picture. Trust that, though you may not be able to see all the details at this point, God does. Believe He can redeem even the darkest situation. Get to know His promises for you and for your future, and then place your trust in Him where it is safe.

Pray for God to open your eyes. Write down your husband's behaviors apart from his good intentions, promises, or explanations. What he *does* is the truth. An addict's words don't mean a thing at this point. The addict wants to keep you in the subjective arena of feelings and emotions. Try to stay in the objective arena of truth. His actions are observable. If he continues in unhealthy behaviors, then he is still unhealthy . . . regardless of the one good thing he might have done last week.

Pray for God to give you *His* heart for your husband. It will take time for those feelings of love to catch up with your decisions. In the meantime, pray for wisdom to know when and where to spend your love. Before further risking your heart, give yourself time to heal and to observe a change of attitude in both yourself and your husband. And from now until forever, let Christ be your first love.

As God reveals a lie to you—about yourself; about your value to Him as a child of God, or to your husband as a wife and lover; about sex, marriage, or anything—write it down and then look for Scriptures that replace that lie with the Truth. A concordance, or topical Bible, or perhaps someone you know who is familiar with the Bible may help you do this. This is a powerful exercise, and I encourage you to do it from this point forward. As you read God's Word, He will continually open your eyes to misconceptions. The only way to combat a lie is with the Truth.

CHAPTER 3

First Shimmers

Seeing the Obstacles

No one gets through life without running up against a few *obstacles*. These hazards are strategically placed by the Father of Lies and are constructed of deceptions. Many lies come from our past experience, misinformation, or our own wrong assumptions. These roadblocks have been added since the time we were children and are a consequence of living in a broken world.

Although some of these obstacles are obvious, which should make them easy to identify, they often go undetected or ignored. A few may even be tucked beneath other objects, out of sight. We have a skillful guide, though, in Christ and an accurate map in His Word. As we get to know both, God gradually makes the hazards visible to us so they can be avoided or replaced with the truth. Step by step the slow and gentle process takes place as we allow God to be our eyes.

The Enemy's lies leave us vulnerable to his schemes and push us off course. When he wants us discouraged, negative, or hopeless, he simply plops a big lie in our path for us to trip over. It can be a dark voice that says things like, "You can't do that," or "Who do you think you are?" Or it might say, "Go ahead, you deserve it," or "A little won't hurt." The Father of Lies goes from telling us, "You are lord of your own life," to "You are worthless." In the arena of lies, there is no consistency—and there are no rules. The Enemy will use whatever works to turn us from what is right, honorable, and good. He's all about keeping our eyes in blinders and our feet tripping over the obstacles.

For some, the most powerful lies are ones that produce fear. For others it's the lies that produce anger or hopelessness or some other dark emotion. When Satan pulls at his thread of lies, we're like puppets on strings, backing away from whatever God is calling us to do. Until the lie behind the emotion is identified, the emotion appears bigger than God. Regardless of how strong our faith or our desire not to be moved, our actions speak louder and to the contrary.

Our eyes can be opened only when we believe, with absolute confidence, that God is all-powerful, merciful, and all-knowing. He alone holds the answers and the plan for our lives. When this powerful truth moves from theory to reality, then there is no fear greater than God. It's important, then, to identify even one lie and recognize its power.

How do we identify lies we're too blind to see? God has to show them to us. Once He opens our eyes to them, we can cut the string of that lie so it no longer has the power to move us. Focusing on the truth keeps us in the hand of God where we belong. Lies, though, take many shapes, and it takes time for us to identify them; it will be a lifelong process. We can be thankful that God is patient.

Tammy was sinking lower and lower into depression, still paralyzed by her pain and stuck in an emotional quicksand.

> I was sure that the problem was me. My self-esteem, which was not very strong to begin with, got even weaker. After the birth of our second child, I spent energy on others and just let myself go. My husband traveled and I stayed home with my two toddlers, so I was usually too busy to think. It seemed all I did was pour myself out to meet everyone else's needs. I thought I was being a good wife and mom. How did

I get to this place? I feel empty and alone, just waiting for my husband's trial and for the results of my blood test to see if I have any STDs. If this isn't the bottom, I don't know what is.

Somewhere along the way, I lost myself. When I felt as though I couldn't even keep my husband's interest sexually, I needed emotional life support. I didn't want anything to do with him, but the thought of life without him was really frightening. There was no way I could provide for my children. I felt trapped, but I couldn't seem to make a decision. I wondered who I was—who I'd become.

Because I couldn't think of anywhere else to turn, I hunted down my old study Bible from college and cracked it open. Reading the Psalms amazed me—this book, written thousands of years ago, was speaking about *my* life. I don't know how long I sat there reading, but I followed the notes from one Scripture to the next until my eyes wouldn't stay open anymore. Reading God's loving words made me think that maybe I could take my first steps and try to climb out of my emotional pit.

Stephanie stepped up her efforts to fix her situation. Even though her husband seemed to be avoiding the problem, she was determined to get help. She put a filter on the computer and then found a support group at a local church. She found a counselor and continued to read books about sexual addiction. This was her surefire method to help her husband.

I was so excited about joining a support group. The first night was powerful. Walking in, I almost stopped short; there were twenty to thirty attractive women. Many, I learned, were college educated. Was I in the right place? Surely women whose husbands struggle with sexual addiction would look dowdy and plain. My thoughts betrayed what I believed. Even after reading more than once that this addiction has nothing to do with attraction, I hadn't accepted it until that moment. Many of those women could have been models.

Leaving that first class, I had hope. The leaders were women who had survived. Surely they could help me fix my husband. I couldn't wait for the next week to learn their secrets.

⁂

As the dust settled around Renee, she began to regret her explosive reactions.

God showed me how out of control I'd been. Yes, I'd been betrayed, but I began to see there was no excuse for my rage and holier-than-thou attitude. And thanks to my big mouth, my husband wasn't the only one who hurt people. I'd let my anger rub off on my two teenage sons, and now they were going through their own hurts. The oldest took my side and was angry with his dad; the younger was just ticked at both of us.

They were also hurt because of my need for revenge. After I first suspected my husband was having an affair, he admitted it right away. He said he was really sorry, but couldn't seem to help himself. He wanted to stop and save our marriage. I was the one who said the marriage was over. Looking back, he seemed really broken up. He even opened up and talked to me about how and why the affair had happened. I rewarded him by yelling at him and telling him what a dog he was. Oh, if only I could have controlled my temper! Instead I kicked him while he was down. No wonder he wanted to be rid of me.

⁂

Getting knocked off course by obstacles begins as soon as we're old enough to understand disappointment. Most people enter marriage already having taken many wrong turns on the general path of life. Betrayal by the one you love brings any positive forward momentum, of course, to a halt. This deep disappointment tends to throw up all kinds of obstacles. It can send us spilling into ditches previously dug by low self-esteem, negative self-talk, prior losses, or abuse. From the bottom of the ditch, the path to healing and health feels completely unattainable.

Tammy's obstacles were the "I'm the problem" lie. Every prior insecure spot became a reason for her problems. The Father of Lies whispered, "You're not productive," "You're not interesting," and "You've let yourself go." She knew for years that she couldn't measure up, so her husband's betrayal merely supported her existing low self-esteem and poor body image, pushing her farther down that well-traveled detour of self-loathing.

Stephanie, on the other hand, found the obstacle marked, "I'm not the problem." The lies she listened to included, "It's all about my husband," "It's up to me to fix him," and "His healing depends on my being a spiritual giant." To her, these lies seemed to direct her journey down a detour of needing to at least appear perfect, and her strong desire for control.

Renee simply believed the lie regarding redheads: she's at the mercy of her anger. Her family and friends reinforced this obstacle every time she blew up. In times of stress, there was only one way she had ever gone—straight to rage.

If "I'm not the problem" and "I am the problem" and "I have no control" are each an obstacle, where does the true path lie? It rests somewhere in the middle. No woman ever caused her husband's sexual addiction. Most men came to their wives already addicted. Nor is anyone completely innocent. We wives come into marriage with our own baggage. Both of these statements are true—and independent of each other. In our brokenness, we enable dysfunction to continue in our home by not recognizing or questioning unhealthy behaviors.

One reason we often don't see these problems is because they're too familiar. It is within our families that we learned how to cope. But if we grew up in a home with poor communication or outbursts of anger, these same behaviors feel familiar and often continue into our marriages. This is why addictions and abuse are typically passed down in families and why unhealthy people find each other and marry. Their behaviors are viewed by each other as normal.

In the face of trauma, falling back on old logic or coping mechanisms is a common response. As children trying to get along in a complex society, we collect the lies that seem to make things bearable or that our parents told us. So our self-esteem, like a house of cards, is fragile, built one lie at a time: "My value comes from my husband, my job, or my looks." It's not surprising that all the cards will tumble when jarred by betrayal or severe trial.

Learning to replace lies with the truth found in God's Word is the only way to rebuild a house that is sturdy enough to withstand the extreme pressures of life. Although rebuilding is not an easy process, there are laws and a blueprint. The first law is a solid foundation— God's immutable truth, which can't be altered and which keeps us grounded. And there are noticeable patterns in truth. False information or wrong assumptions tend to lean toward discouragement, while the truth installs walls, rooms, and windows of hope. Also, most lies keep us tied to the past or things we can't change, while the truth focuses on the future, promoting positive change. When God speaks, He clears up any confusion about what is lie and what is truth, which provides a sense of peace even in the face of difficulty. And the more we know about our heavenly Father, the clearer His voice becomes.

Hearing the truth is not, of course, always painless, but it brings freedom. We no longer feel like a victim of our circumstances. We learn to read not only our own emotions but learn why others react the way they do. Recognizing this cause and effect helps us to identify the thoughts to ignore, which are based in lies, as well as those to heed, which are based in truth. In heeding or ignoring those readings, the battle will be won—or lost—in our minds long before we act.

This process of becoming aware does get easier over time. As Tammy began to fill her mind with more of God's Word, the truth started to shimmer, like the "Path Lights" at the end of these chapters, making it easier for her to recognize. The Bible spoke directly to her lies while shedding light on the hope she thought was lost. Every time shimmers of truth were added, her path became clearer, her steps became surer, and her future became more beautiful.

If Stephanie will allow God to change her, and if she works at knowing the truth, the impact will be profound. It's sad, but right now she's putting her energy in the wrong place, trying to fix her husband. Setting out to change him will not help her to heal or grow. She must trust God to work on her husband, and use all the energy she's spending on him to ask God to change her.

We have more impact on others, after all, when *we* change. It's called leading by example. When people see what God has done in our lives, it becomes easier for them to believe He can do it in theirs. Even if those around us don't change, God becomes our focus and we are stronger and healthier for it. We know where we're going because He is leading the way in truth. And there is power in truth. I will be like a parrot repeating this point because it's critical. God's truth identifies what our responsibilities really are and are not. In Renee's case, she was so focused on her husband's betrayal that she couldn't see straight, and she thought she was in control. Her anger was a way of avoiding her responsibility. As long as she was focused on what her husband did, she didn't have to look inward or answer for her poor response.

A lot of Christian women, including me, believe a very subtle lie. We're taught that to be Christlike we should serve others and surrender. But this is only part of the picture—one half of the truth. We *are* called to serve, but not without having proper boundaries. Otherwise we end up becoming overly responsible. I had all kinds of "godly" reasons for not setting boundaries, one of which was to "keep the peace." When God showed me that my attempt to keep the peace was enabling others to remain unhealthy, my eyes were opened to the truth. When, for instance, I stopped reacting to my husband's anger, he was left alone to deal with it himself. Simply removing myself from the equation changed everything. I didn't have to put up with his outbursts in order to be a good, Christlike wife.

Lies like the "surrender without boundaries" one are often only a hair off due north on the compass of truth, but a fraction is still too much. Anyone who's ever used a real compass knows that being even a little off course is too much. The farther you travel, the farther off course you get from the correct destination.

When I don't set boundaries, I pave the way for others to sin. I fell into this snare by taking responsibility for things such as others' decisions and feelings. I was quick to assume all responsibility for any conflict: "If I were only less selfish or more patient, there wouldn't be a problem." Then I'd turn around and not take responsibility for my choices, emotions, or reactions: "You make me so mad." These are a few of the lies that trip us and make us fall flat, and instead of being a servant, we become a doormat. Christ modeled servanthood but He was never a doormat.

As God opened my eyes to my lack of boundaries, all of my relationships grew healthier. I became a better friend. My "yes" meant exactly that and my "no" was definite. There was a great deal of comfort in knowing what responsibility was mine and what wasn't. It was so freeing to realize I'm responsible only for my own feelings and choices. One friendship didn't survive because when I stopped taking responsibility for her moods and the behaviors that resulted from them, she couldn't handle it, couldn't accept responsibility for herself. I now know it's better to lose an unhealthy friendship than to lose myself in the process of trying to keep it.

If Tammy, for instance, were any more selfless, she might disappear altogether. Of course this warped thinking was her responsibility since she believed the lies. Healing could begin once she found the truth—that she did have choices and that making the wise ones was her responsibility. She was stuck as long as she made excuses for the broken places—"I let myself go"; "He needs to blow off steam"—or, worse, learned to live with them because it was easier than accepting her own responsibility—"I wore rose-colored glasses"; "I didn't have boundaries with my husband and kids."

My faults and failures no longer scare me. They're opportunities to grow. Making mistakes and poor choices are simply reminders that God gave us free will to make our own way. At some point every person makes bad choices, because we all sin. Yet we can be thankful that God is just and merciful. Though the consequence for sin is separation from God and eternal death, He made sure there was another way to cross over into relationship with Him. Since I can't be holy, and because God can't look upon my sin, Christ's blood is needed to cover me—to pay the debt I never could. There is no other way. All the good words I could muster would never make up for my sin. This revelation brought renewed thanks to God for sending His Son to die on my behalf.

As I contemplated this truth, I realized something profound. Seeing how God loves me changed the way I viewed my husband, others, and myself. God showed me that my guilt wasn't any more forgivable than my husband's, or anyone else's for that matter. My poor choices, no matter their ramifications, were just as disappointing to God. When someone misses a mark, it doesn't matter by how much. Lifting my perspective, I saw that from the vantage point of heaven, my sin required the same price as my husband's—Christ's suffering, blood, and life. Really seeing every person as broken leveled the playing field. This was a sobering and humbling realization.

This was not new information, but my heart had never fully grasped the significance. I knew that good works—doing all the "right" stuff, church attendance, giving, serving, and praying—isn't what saves me. But, detoured by my obstacles of lies, I assumed they would keep me safe: *Surely if I'm a godly and loving wife, I will never have to worry about being betrayed.* How subtle the lies are. Did God owe me anything? Hadn't He already given me everything I would ever need in the death and resurrection of His only Son? Yet I expected more. I got on my knees and asked God for forgiveness the moment I saw how selfish I'd been. How thankful I am that His grace is sufficient, indeed.

The Enemy, of course, jumped in and tried to convince me that I was unworthy. And while I acknowledge that I am flawed, my being flawed was only part of the truth. The other part is that I am redeemed through Christ. Without the rest of the truth, I could be kept from approaching the throne of grace, barred by my flaws. I owe thanks to God that I know the end of the story. God's grace is simply this—unmerited favor. I do not deserve it, but it flowed out of His holy character and has nothing to do with me.

Now the good works that I do come only from a heart overflowing with gratitude and not a need to earn God's love. I have more than I can ever comprehend already—we all do. The only requirement is that we see and accept the gift. Then we need to surrender our old map for the road of life and let God show us a new one—step by step.

The wonderful thing about truth is that it never changes. It's like an amazing and incorruptible solid slab upon which God laid the foundations of the world. It never shifts or erodes. Christ knew He would be the sacrificial lamb, and our Triune God's plan was in place before the world was created. Every man, woman, and child would be made to worship Him. The Old Testament points to it and the New Testament documents it. Each person must, then, decide what to do about the plan—Jesus' death for our salvation. Nothing we do changes or impacts that plan. All we can do is decide to accept it or reject it.

God also has a perfect plan for every life; we decide to accept or reject it. If we accept His plan, then we let His loving hand gently guide the direction and gently identify the pitfalls in every area of life. Being open to God's straightening of our twisted thinking is an ongoing challenge.

After betrayal, step one on the path to healing is surrendering to His care. Another significant step for me was meeting with a godly Christian counselor who had experience working with issues of sexual addiction. Finding someone who knew the common pitfalls was helpful. This "good" Christian counselor was a powerful addition to the help given me in the support group. A Christian counselor was essential for me because I don't know how a person works through the pain of betrayal without divine intervention and help. I didn't want to waste time and money on someone who was not pointing me back to God and truth.

I will say at this point that not all counselors are the same. A counselor's being Christian isn't even a guarantee that he or she will point you to the right path. So, consult your pastor and/or another godly leader. Pray before you go, and then trust your instincts. If you're not comfortable with the first counselor, try another. It's also essential that the counselor has experience dealing with issues related to sexual addiction. Get a referral if at all possible.

At first I had the idea that going to a counselor meant that there was something wrong with me. Putting my pride aside enabled me to see what a valuable tool it was. Counseling provided a place to go more deeply into my personal experiences than was possible in the support group. Applying the concepts I was learning in the group to my situation, using the help of an objective counselor, sped up my healing process. The counselor would ask me the tough questions, helping me identify many remaining lies.

The right counselor will point you back to Christ. Mine did, and I love how faithfully and patiently God helped me identify one wrong thought or assumption at a time. Each revelation strengthened my stance, helping me maneuver the obstacles of lies, taking my feet from the sand and placing them on The Rock. In the same way a new relationship deepens after it survives the first storm, my relationship with Christ grew. I saw how much God loved me—flaws and all. He loved me too much to let me stay unhealthy. Neither the good nor the bad things I did affected Him. Jesus was intimately in tune, in love, and interested in me.

The process of finding my obstacles will go on throughout my life. Identifying the tactics of the Enemy is easy to miss as he twists the truth bit by bit. The more time I spend in God's Word and in prayer, the easier to identify the obstacles of lies and to recognize when I'm going off on a wrong detour. I also see that staying this divine course is sometimes too difficult for me to go it alone. I need God's people. And because my healing has promoted healthiness in my family, they, too, come along beside me.

Many of these glimmers from this chapter are additional rays of hope. Here is a quick review.

- I need help on this journey.
- Only God can change my heart.
- No one is righteous, not one.

- Christ died that I would truly live.
- God loves me without limits.

Path Lights

There's not one totally good person on earth,
not one who is truly pure and sinless.
(Eccl. 7:20)

People with their minds set on you,
    you keep completely whole,
steady on their feet,
    because they keep at it and don't quit.
(Isa. 26:3)

This is how much God loved the world: He gave his Son, his
one and only Son. And this is why: so that no one need be
destroyed; by believing in him, anyone can have a whole and
lasting life. (John 3:16)

Then you will experience for yourselves the truth, and the
truth will free you. (John 8:32)

We use our powerful God-tools for smashing warped phi-
losophies, tearing down barriers erected against the truth of
God, fitting every loose thought and emotion and impulse
into the structure of life shaped by Christ. (2 Cor. 10:5)

Whatever I have, wherever I am, I can make it through anything in the One who makes me who I am. (Phil. 4:13)

Journaling

As you journal, write down any lies that God has brought to your
mind, and that you may have identified as you read this chapter. As

you read all the above Scriptures, see if they help you identify any lies. Most of all, pray that the Holy Spirit will shed light on all additional lies, then look through God's Word for the truths that remove the lies. All this writing about lies should become part of all of your journaling from now on. This may feel like a waste of time or even silly—that's a lie. Learning to identify lies is the single most important tool you will have. It's like learning to use the stars to navigate. How can you find true north without it?

CHAPTER 4

Lanterns

Safe People

I call them *lanterns*—because they are mentors who shed light. As the process of looking out for obstacles continues, you'll find that your desire grows for God and for truth. As the Lord reveals additional obstacles, He graciously provides people who also see pitfalls and roadblocks that we might otherwise miss. God uses others who are ahead of us on the path to shine a light to help us. They're living proof that two are better than one. When we're in a weakened state, it's important to be surrounded by people who are safe and who provide biblically sound advice that points us in the right direction.

Allowing others to see that we are visually impaired makes us vulnerable. So it's essential to approach possible lanterns carefully and slowly. Beware the tendency of being too open—sharing indiscriminately—as well as being too closed off—not sharing at all. Both delay healing. Just let God identify the right people and the proper timing, because the wrong person can cause more damage, while the right one can be a craftsman of God. I've met many women who can attest to the damage wrought by the wrong person.

Tammy had started to feel relief from her pain. The more time she spent in God's Word, the more hope she found. She could see the light of God's face again even through all the pain that her husband's behavior had caused both of them. Christ's love wasn't a theory—it was real.

I really needed to see progress, and I was ready to take care of me. It was like someone waking me up. My only desire was to experience God's love in a deeper, more personal, way. I felt even more hopeful after getting the results back of my blood tests—they came back clear.

I decided to join a women's Bible study group at my church, but I began to have doubts about that decision from the first day. Initially I thought the group leader was knowledgable. I soon realized, though, that she always had an answer for every question and never really allowed others to share their own thoughts. My doubts proved to be well founded.

The first time I hinted of trouble in my marriage, she pounced. She zeroed in on me and started asking a lot of probing and personal questions. She gave me the impression that I needed fixing, and that she thought she was the one to do it. I haven't gone back since. It seemed as though my rose-colored glasses had been replaced with fear and distrust and anger. I long to go back to the days of blissful ignorance.

Stephanie continued in her support group. As she gradually felt safe, she began to share about her husband's computer porn habit and all of her own research. These women understood her pain and her desire to help her husband. Many had walked similar paths.

I don't know if I can put into words how amazing it was to hear other women tell their stories. As each person shared how they found out about their husband's addiction and the tidal wave of emotions that followed, my feelings of isolation melted. Having never been in a group that was so "real" before, it was refreshing. Every story, although unique, had some point of connection, something I could relate to.

One story in particular got to me. This woman's experience started differently than mine, but when she started to share her obsession with checking on her husband, my heart started to pound. She described how she had checked credit card statements, phone bills, his desk drawers, and listened in on his phone conversations. She confessed her need to be in control—and I saw myself.

We were a diverse group in many ways. The leader's words and actions set a tone of acceptance and confidentiality. I knew from the first day that there would be no condemnation nor pat answers. It was hard to let down my guard, but feeling safe and understood helped me to be vulnerable.

The ladies even began to challenge my desire to fix my husband. They gently explained that he was the only one responsible for his own healing. This truth wasn't easy to hear, but I trusted their input. Understanding brought a flood of new questions. If my husband wasn't willing to do the work, where did that leave me? And what am I responsible for?

I'm going to continue with this group and pray they can answer my questions.

❧

Renee decided it was time to take some positive steps in order to prevent further damage to herself and her family. Her volatile temper had already done enough damage and could cost her marriage.

My pastor recommended a Christian counselor he thought I should see. The first meeting was emotionally draining but we went right to the core issues. She helped me to see my selfish and destructive behavior as separate from my husband's. Nothing he did could ever justify my not being accountable for my own responses. I didn't want to agree with that at first because it was painful to realize. I always felt I was in the right when I lashed out at my husband.

Week by week my counselor and I looked back at my childhood to see why it was so easy for me to respond in anger. The whole process made me feel emotionally drained, and to be honest, I wanted to be angry with the counselor— but I knew she was right.

Then after a couple of months, my counselor asked me to think about writing letters of apology to my sons, family members, and husband. Writing those letters was really hard because I had to admit my responsibility in the whole mess, and it wasn't easy. It was like reliving the pain. After several drafts and a lot of arguing with myself, my feelings finally caught up with the truth.

God began to change my heart. It was a start. And my counselor is helping me find "the space" between a bad situation and my angry reaction. I never realized I had a choice on how to react.

My husband asked me to meet him for dinner. I was a nervous wreck. After all those weeks, I wasn't sure what to expect. Even after I'd prayed for his forgiveness, I knew he might be asking me to meet him so he could ask for the signed divorce papers. Without my anger force field, I felt vulnerable. Thankfully, I knew God would be with me. Trusting Him for the strength to get through each day made it possible to hope.

❧

Moving forward in our healing will, at some point, mean letting others in. The first and safest step you can take is to tell God all about it. It's time to stop pretending He doesn't already know what you're thinking and feeling. Once you've bared your soul to Him, then move on to telling others as appropriate. God's Word makes it clear that we're not meant to be individual islands. He calls us to meet together, to encourage one another, and to confess to other believers our struggles. He designed us to be in community and understands the meaning of synergy, the benefit of combined effort and operation.

Pray for God to direct this important step of finding mentors. For some, the seemingly natural step of going to their pastors turned out to cause new pain. The pastors may have been condemners, accusers, fixers, or all three. Pastors are not perfect; they are people, as are counselors. So if you're disappointed by someone you thought would prove to be a good mentor, don't give up. Moving forward as God directs is the best path, and then trust your gut. If something doesn't feel right, get another opinion from someone you trust.

God speaks in many ways, through His Word, His Spirit, and often His children. Christ, who surely could have worked alone, invited twelve men to share in His ministry while He was on earth. He was teaching them by example, which is still our model for today. The disciples knew Jesus was a man of His word and that He loved them. They welcomed His teaching and even His discipline at times. God has placed in each of us a desire for this type of loving fellowship. There is nothing more encouraging than a loving word of affirmation from someone who knows our hearts.

Tammy was ready to receive some healthy input to speed up her recovery. It's sad that she got started in the wrong place, and if she'd stayed there, it was inevitable that she would have been injured further. It's essential to have a safe environment that offers a Christlike balance of truth and love. But what is fundamental to look for in a mentor? When deciding if a person or group is safe, the first step is always prayer. The Holy Spirit is able to give amazing insight. Next, look for people who are

- nonjudgmental (they don't decide, they guide);
- respectful (they set and observe healthy boundaries);
- spiritual (they point to Christ not to pat religious answers);
- listeners (they really hear you);
- objective (they're able to give and receive loving criticism);
- humble (they know when to say, "I don't know").

Safe people will not condemn you or your husband. They understand that we're all imperfect in the eyes of God. They should give and expect respect, which comes from an understanding that everyone is valuable in the eyes of God. These kinds of mentors are spiritual instead of religious, which means they not only know the letter of God's law, they understand the nature of His love. Spiritual people rely on God's wisdom, not their own, and this makes them good listeners. They understand that listening is more important than talking, and that asking questions is more valuable than giving answers. And listening and asking questions is a sign of an objective person, as well as a humble person. Humble people ask questions because they know they don't have all the answers. They haven't confused *knowing the One* who has all the answers with knowing all the answers themselves.

So where do you find safe people when it seems so easy to find the unhealthy? In truth, with God's help they get easier to find. At the risk of being repetitive, the best place to start is with prayer. The hard part is to patiently wait for God to identify these safe people. When we're looking for a lantern to shine some light on this path of obstacles, pitfalls, and roadblocks, it's difficult to wait for a person to reveal his or her character. But this wait reduces the chance of trying to read our maps under a wavering light, while reminding us first to place our lives under God's steady light. The best way to avoid additional injury is to move slowly and always talk to God before you talk to others.

Once Tammy recognized that her Bible study leader was not respecting her privacy, she did the right thing in leaving. Tammy could have stayed and had a word with the leader about her manner, but given the situation, Tammy is not responsible to fix her leader. Also, constructive criticism is helpful only when there is mutual trust between the helper and the hurting person. But a person who pries into areas where she has not been invited is not a safe person, regardless of how pure she thinks her motives are.

Stephanie was fortunate to find a group of people who not only respected her boundaries but also shared similar trials. This respect and common experience is what makes a support group different from, say, a fellowship or study group. People working together through a common difficulty encourage each other, because experience sometimes teaches in a way that textbook expertise cannot. Who better to understand our journey than those who are on a similar path?

As I look back over the past few years, I'm amazed at God's faithfulness in providing me with many safe people as well as cotravelers. I'm humbled by the time and energy that these shining lanterns invested in my husband, our girls, and me. Now, as a facilitator of the support group at my church, I have the privilege of passing on that same comfort and support to others. I place each new group in the hands of Christ and then wait for Him to show me what to do.

The hearts of the women in these groups are exposed and vulnerable. All of our hearts are, or have been, in this place. As our paths merge with the paths of other travelers, God may redirect us in order for us to preserve our boundaries. I've mentioned boundaries a lot, how important they are, and the necessity of having healthy limits. I didn't always have an accurate understanding of what healthy boundaries are. That's the unfortunate result of the way most of us learned to cope as children. If we didn't see boundaries modeled, chances are we don't have any, or we put up walls instead.

Boundaries are limits or borders that outline a person's ownership and responsibility. Imagine a garden full of vegetables and flowers. The gardener works on her flower and vegetable beds—planting, weeding, watering, and harvesting. As she labors, visitors stop by. Some are welcome; some are unwelcome. The welcome visitors respect the garden bed—they're careful not to tread on plants, they ask relevant questions about the flowers and vegetables, they may even identify and pull out a weed or two while they chat. The unwelcome visitors are careless about where they step; they pluck flowers without asking; they point out that the tomatoes look small.

To keep the unwelcome visitors outside the garden, the gardener needs to have a fence, a boundary. The fence needs a gate to let in the welcome visitors, and the gate needs to have a lock on the inside to keep out those who do not respect the garden and the crops. Notice that the gardener doesn't build a wall. Unwelcome visitors may stop by and look at the flowers and vegetables, but the boundary keeps the beds from being trampled and the flowers from being taken. The gardener decides who can join her in the garden, who must stay outside, and whom to share her flowers and vegetables with. With the boundary, her space is protected and she's in control of it. As she shares and chats with her welcome visitors, they both benefit. This is a good visual for me to remember how I should treat my heart and its contents.

Tammy set an appropriate boundary by not returning to a group that threatened to cause her more damage. Stephanie opened her heart to her support group only after they had shown their respect of her, proven they were trustworthy, and agreed to share from their own hearts. They encouraged her to concentrate on her own garden and step out of her husband's until she was invited. These words were not easy for Stephanie to hear, but she knew she could trust the speakers based on the fruitful harvest she had observed in their lives. Renee realized that she needed to apologize to several people whose gardens she had trampled through. She took responsibility and was willing to do any repair work God called her to do.

While our boundaries define what our responsibilities are and are not, they shouldn't prevent us from receiving constructive advice. If we close ourselves off, which is not uncommon after betrayal, chances are we've built a brick wall instead of a picket fence with a gate. Nothing, good or bad, gets in—or out.

A betrayal can be a wake-up call that we need to set up those boundaries. By the time of discovery, our gardens have already been trampled, and the betrayal has left the garden in the darkness of a perpetual night, without a single ray of sunlight. What we need is a lantern in the garden. God's lanterns, those mentors He brings across our paths, not only help illuminate the obstacles along the path of healing, but they can also shine light into our gardens.

Once we are sure these people have our best interests in mind and trust has been established, we can allow them inside the garden gate. These divine workers shine light on the injured areas and help us understand that they can be healed. They help reveal destructive vines that we thought were harmless.

There are obstacles when we repair the garden, too. It can be both discouraging and painful when we find debris—stuff we thought we'd deeply buried but has now percolated up and is lying just below the top soil. And letting others into the process can be even more difficult. But experienced gardeners—those mentors who are the lanterns—know about plants that have been trampled; often, when the damaged parts are removed, the plants can heal. Then they are that much hardier and, in time, yield more bountiful blossoms and produce.

When it comes to finding your lanterns, take it slowly, pray through the process, and let God help you erect appropriate boundaries. When God used others in my reworking process, it was both humbling and awe inspiring. I'd never felt more loved, valued, and cared for. What's more, God used me to do similar repairs in the lives of others. The blessings continue to grow and produce a beautiful harvest.

Additional glimmers that are my rays of hope:

- Trust the Holy Spirit working in you.
- I am not defined by others' opinions.
- Not all friends are created equal.
- God will provide people to support me.
- I'm responsible only for my own garden.

Path Lights

The teaching of the wise is a fountain of life,
    so, no more drinking from death-tainted wells!
    (Prov. 13:14)

By yourself you're unprotected.
With a friend you can face the worst.
Can you round up a third?
A three-stranded rope is not easily snapped.
    (Eccl. 4:12)

All praise to the God and Father of our Master, Jesus the Messiah! Father of all mercy! God of all healing counsel! He comes alongside us when we go through hard times, and before you know it, he brings us alongside someone else who is going through hard times so that we can be there for that person just as God was there for us. (2 Cor. 1:3–4)

Make a careful exploration of who you are and the work you have been given, and then sink yourself into that. Don't be impressed with yourself. Don't compare yourself with others. Each of you must take responsibility for doing the creative best you can with your own life. (Gal. 6:4–5)

Stick with me, friends. Keep track of those you see running this same course, headed for the same goal. There are many out there taking other paths, choosing other goals, and trying to get you to go along with them. (Phil. 3:17–18)

Journaling

Take some time to look at past relationships, both the positive and the painful ones. Start by writing down relationships that have ended, and ask God to reveal any unhealthiness or patterns that were present in them. As with the previous chapter, look for any lies driving your behavior. Ask Him to reveal any unresolved issues that need to be addressed. Are there any situations you need to take responsibility for? Or do you see yourself taking on the responsibilities of others?

Now look at your current ties. Are they healthy? Do both you and the other people involved participate and invest equally in the relationship? Are there any relationships that need to go? Again, pray for God to guide this process of examination or of correcting the balance in a current relationship. The reality, however, is that as you become healthier and set appropriate boundaries, it will likely cause friction with those who don't have boundaries or who don't respect them.

Finally, ask God to reveal one person you can count on for support. Watch for a mentor or someone who is farther on in their life's journey. Pray for someone who will encourage spiritual growth. Always be looking for people who have character qualities you admire. Then pray for God to open a door for the relationship to go forward.

CHAPTER 5

Laser

Friend or Foe

A *laser* is a highly concentrated ray of light. Used correctly, it can promote healing, cleanly and precisely cutting away dangerous growths. Used incorrectly, it can destroy everything in its path. Anger is much like a laser. Righteous anger can be healing when it springs from pure truth and is motivated by love. Take away that pure mixture by adding a half-truth, a hidden motive, a pinch of fear or pride, and the result will be hurtful instead healing.

Because of the power of anger, most people either avoid it or misuse it. As a result, anger has a poor reputation. Anger is not inherently bad. The Bible records Jesus as having been angry on occasion. Both the Pharisees and money changers felt His ire. Christ even tossed over a few tables, yet He is without sin. How can this be? We don't spend much time studying the anger of God, but we don't read far into the book of Genesis before realizing that God became angry with His children—and rightly so. He desires and deserves to be Lord of our life, and He is angry when we put other people or things first.

Since we aren't God, we must carefully look at how our anger differs from His. In order to get to the core of our anger, we must look at our hearts because "Out of the overflow of his heart his mouth speaks" (Luke 6:45 NIV). Motive for anger, then, is the key to its core. Our problem is that we're often blind to underlying motives. In order to respond with appropriate anger, rather than react impulsively, we need to stop and invite God into our anger. A few moments of restraint can prevent lasting and devastating consequences.

On the other hand, if we avoid anger altogether by stuffing, denying, or bypassing it, we harm ourselves. We all know someone who does this. She's the "sweetest person I know and doesn't have an angry hair on her head." What you may not see is the pain this person carries. Some people keep all their anger inside until they're physically ill. Others express their anger through backdoor tactics like being passive-aggressive. A passive-aggressive wife, for example, might act like nothing's wrong while she's with her husband but then do something malicious to him behind his back.

One way that women, especially, avoid anger is to talk themselves out of it: "After all, in the scheme of things, it really isn't that important"; "If I'm to be a good Christian, then I need to give in to others." This feels like grace, but it's really unresolved anger. The problem is, anger doesn't go away; it tends to ooze out in other ways. A woman may yell at the people she loves for no reason, or carry around little resentments like a bag of pebbles. She doesn't even realize that others can hear her pebbles rattling when she speaks. Some women are so afraid of their anger and keep it so well hidden that no one knows the pain, shame, and guilt they carry.

What these women don't realize is that we all get mad. It's a God-given emotion. Anger has a purpose. It's a warning light. It's designed to tell us that some other emotion is out of balance and needs to be corrected. Its flashing tells us to look deeper and see what is wrong.

Anger has three possible triggers—shame (embarrassment), pain (injury/loss), and helplessness (lack of control). Once we find the real cause of our anger, then we can address that core issue with an appropriate response—which may well include anger.

At this point I would be remiss if I didn't mention the dangerous side of anger—abuse. I want to be clear on this point. Anger that's used to control, manipulate, and hold another emotionally hostage is out of control and abusive. It typically starts with name-calling, emotional jabs at a person's self-worth, painful teasing, public insults. It progresses from there. Eventually the abuser is yelling, grabbing, pushing, slapping, and becoming increasingly aggressive and violent. Remorse follows. So too does more abuse. Even just one of these tactics is abuse, and it won't stop without serious intervention. If you or your children are being treated in this fashion, *please* seek help. If you are not sure, but you think you might be in an abusive relationship—you probably are! Please take the following steps in moving forward.

- Get help today! Tell someone—your pastor, counselor, or call for help. Check your local listings under Domestic Abuse, Women's Crisis Services, or Social Services.
- Do not confront your abuser alone.
- Have a plan (the above organizations can help).
- Don't make excuses; your life is at risk. It will not go away or get better on its own.

॰ॐ॰

All four women, including me, in our support group experienced anger at the initial discovery of our husbands' betrayal. Tammy's negative experience with the Bible study only strengthened the grip of anger that threatened to knock her into another detour. Then new layers of pain were added as she tried to move forward. She wondered if there was anyone she could depend on.

> I couldn't believe that a churchwoman could be so pushy. I wondered, "Where is God? Isn't there anyone I can depend on?" I was afraid to confront the group leader or to go to any other group, and I didn't want to go out of the house, so sleeping was my out. The still small voice said, "Get up," but I didn't respond. I couldn't remember what a normal day looked like.
>
> My husband seemed to be existing in a different world

than mine. Living in the same house with each other but without connecting was worse than being alone. Because I was never sure of where he was, I assumed he was still into his addiction. He wasn't getting help, and instead, he blamed me. When we did talk, he pointed his finger as I absorbed his guilt.

Then I'd think of all the times I scrimped, saved, and cut coupons while my husband was spending money on God knows what. Then when he was caught, it cost $500 to get his car back from the police and $1,000 for a lawyer. All I could think of was how he never spent any money on me. It all just made me more and more angry. I was angry at my husband and at myself.

I wrestled with all my emotions and when I had enough, I decided to let the anger move me forward. I was tired of feeling like a victim who had no choices. Someone had to make the first step. I knew something had to change, so I prayed about it. Then an idea came to mind. I wrote out a detailed plan. Somehow making a plan—where I'd go and how to best take care of the kids—gave me strength. I looked at my finances, opened a bank account in my name only, and searched out possible career fields. Each decision gave me more confidence. I felt God encouraging me to depend on Him alone. He gave me a strength I never had on my own.

Then I felt ready to make another decision: my husband could no longer treat me poorly. I told him in a calm voice that he'd have to leave and couldn't come back until he made some significant change. If he refused, I'd take the kids and go. This was the first time I'd ever stood up for myself—we were both surprised. It felt good not to be controlled by his outbursts, and I didn't have to get angry. I simply said the truth. I could feel God providing the support as I watched him pack.

Stephanie continued to blossom and grow in her support group. Week by week she found her own glimmers of hope. Her focus had shifted from her husband to helping herself heal.

> We wrote an anger letter this week. It was more difficult than I anticipated it would be. Swirling thoughts rushed into my mind, out of the pen, and onto the page. Even after addressing many lies in the support group, there was more to process. I discovered, even as I wrote, the buried anger at my husband for all that was lost: intimacy, dreams, friendships, and the years. They could not be retrieved.
>
> I was angry with God, but ashamed and afraid to admit it. Then one of the other ladies dared to say the words out loud. When lightning didn't zap her, I was able to express my own anger and find freedom, not condemnation. Of course God already knew I was angry with Him, but I had to face my own anger—much like a child needs to face the monster under the bed. I needed to look under there and see the truth—that there was no monster. I shared with the group how much I was learning.
>
> Then the leader really challenged me. She asked, "Would you say you're guided by God or by your intellect?" We all knew the answer. The pregnant pause gave birth to the hard reality—I didn't like anything that didn't seem logical. I knew in that moment that if I was going to go the next step with Christ, I had to let go of needing a definite destination and detailed directions.

Renee is testing her newfound boundaries, enjoying freedom from her angry outbursts. She followed through with her counselor's assignment of taking responsibility for her actions and reactions.

> I met with a few family members to apologize—and I got varied results. My sister-in-law, for example, wasn't ready to

let go of her anger—I didn't blame her. But learning that her reaction was not my responsibility helped. It was still hard, but I saw myself in her. Anger is a good way to keep others at bay.

Our sons' reactions were the opposite of each other's. My youngest wanted to let go of his anger at his dad, while the oldest remained protective of me. As we talked, I could see that the oldest couldn't let go of his anger until he saw me fully let go of my anger. Otherwise forgiving his dad would feel like betraying me. I assured my son that his dad wasn't a villain. He's a good man who made a bad choice. My sons and I cried together, and I could feel the resentment falling away and peace begin filling our home.

God called me to speak the truth in love and to apologize. Any reactions, positive or negative, belonged to the people having them. That was harder to accept when the reactions were negative. I saw my old ways in their anger, and I was tempted to get defensive.

Now I'm recognizing the difference that owning my own reactions makes, and it keeps me from being a slave to my rage. My husband even responded to my new attitude. We decided not to make any more rash decisions but to each work on our own stuff for now.

He's broken all ties to the other woman and is seeing a counselor. I'm still wrestling with my anger at the other woman—but I can at least feel sorry for her. If I were ever to see her, I'm not sure I could find the space before I react badly. This is a tough one for me. God is the only one who can change my heart, and I'm still asking. But at least there's a crack in my armor.

❧

Anger is complex. It can be used to get others off track because it derails most conversations and puts people on the defensive. And though it's not the primary emotion, it can take on a life of its own. Anger actually comes out of deeper emotions that are harder to identify and own. Remember, anger is often the result of hurt, embarrassment, or helplessness, but an angry person rarely addresses the core issue. He or she doesn't see that the boiling geyser really springs from deeper feelings. They only see red.

God created all of our emotions with purposes. In the same way that pain from touching a hot stove tells us to move our hand, feeling emotional pain should tell us to move. Our anger should be a yellow warning light. Its flashing should cause us to look at our circumstances carefully and make a change or get help. More often, rage is a red light identifying a pending explosion. Taking the warning, getting all the facts, and finding the truth will ensure an appropriate response instead of an inappropriate reaction.

It's hard to imagine our being able to think about appropriate responses when we're so angry we want to explode. What many women don't realize is that there's a space between the emotion and the response. I used to say to others, "You make me so mad." Then I learned the truth. "I make me so mad." I decide. So how do I decide not to be angry? I have to choose to stop. One way is to process my emotions on paper first (then put the paper in the shredder). When I take time out to think through the issue I'm angry over, the pause keeps my feelings from controlling the situation and prevents further damage.

Another pause is as simple as telling the other person, "I'll have to get back to you while I take the time I need to calm down." We must be sure to get back, however, and deal with the person—otherwise nothing is resolved. We've avoided the anger but found no solution.

Replacing one unhealthy response—exploding—with another—avoiding—is not the goal. The goal is to use the space between anger and response for turning to God for guidance. Tammy hated confrontation, and she'd say, "I need to think about it," then never bring it up again. Defeated by her husband's explosive anger and blame, she felt powerless. Her coping strategy was avoidance. If she didn't express her feelings, then her husband couldn't jump on them. She needed to set a boundary with him, but that would fuel his rage. Then she started using her "thinking it over" space to hand over her anger to God. Once she did that, she realized that as long as she feared the anger of others, she would be ruled by them. God used that space to move her forward in her understanding, and she no longer felt as powerless.

Stephanie was realizing her anger was disguised as rationalizing. She would debate to the death in order to change a mind, and she had an answer for everything. Once Stephanie implemented use of her space, she realized her tactics convinced no one, and it pushed people away. She decided to stop trying to change others and let God change her—and it made all the difference. Experiencing the power of speaking the truth, in love, was freeing. It liberated her from the burden of proof, and instead of hitting others over the head with statistics and expert opinion, she realized honest communication could stand alone. A loving truth works in a way that arguing never can. Stephanie saw that God didn't need her to defend His truth, but He did want her to fully rely on Him.

Now when her husband reacts poorly, she remains silent or calmly restates the truth. She no longer feels the impulse to convince him. Then he's left to wrestle alone with God and the truth. She found that the conversation was less likely to get off track this way. In the past, she would react to her husband's angry response, and as she was berating his poor behavior, they both spun away from the original issue.

Renee used to think it was healthy to "let off steam" either at the antagonist or with a friend. In reality, this only served to stir the pot to boiling, especially if her comrade agreed with her even when she was wrong. In her rage, stopping to consider the consequences of her wrath never crossed her mind. Once she inserted her space and trusted in God, the reality of where her anger had taken her dawned on her, and she continued in her damage control. Renee is committed to looking for the truth even if she doesn't like it. Now she has a plan to ensure that she makes a space; desiring God's perspective, she prays before she speaks.

I discovered, too, that getting to the core emotions with the help of the Holy Spirit is the best way to find the truth. Early in my healing process, I was driving to a meeting and realized I'd forgotten to bring a hole-punch. One of the ladies left it at my house the last time we met. I went ballistic. I was in full rage and in tears over a hole-punch. Once I got into my space and calmed down, I realized how out of proportion my emotions were. God gently showed me that my rage was displaced. My anger had nothing to do with an inanimate object—it went much deeper. My strong feelings of pain, shame, and helplessness were rolling at the bottom of my boiling cauldron of anger. They could be identified only when the waters were calm, and removing them could only happen by the long arm of God.

I've seen the sad tendency of hurting women to hold onto anything familiar rather than risk the unknown by trusting in God. Fear of change can keep us tied to our pain. One woman in the support group wrapped herself in suffering like it was an old coat. She seemed to enjoy the sympathy and status of being a victim. In some ways it feels easier to be a victim because it takes virtually no thought or effort. Working through change, on the other hand, is arduous at first, but by avoiding the work, this woman was missing out on the chance to gain a measure of control over her situation. A feeling of control would allow her to stand up and fling off her victimhood and feel the warmth of the sun, free of her heavy burden.

Our past experiences can also keep us from fully trusting God. Each time I was faced with the opportunity to grab onto the Lord's hand, the Enemy reminded me of past disappointments—times when my husband, a pastor, or a friend had let me down. The memory of that pain and the feeling that I was invisible to God left me frozen with fear. Why should I trust God when everyone else has lied? The answer was in the question: Why should I trust God? Because everyone else has lied. I could place my full trust in Jesus Christ because He is the only One who has never let me down and could never forsake me. He can't—it goes against His perfect nature.

Once I fully grasped this truth, the world changed. I no longer expected the important people in my life to be perfect. When those people failed, as we all inevitably do, my more realistic expectations allowed me to extend grace instead of justifying the failure. I'm learning, too, not to set people up for failure by putting them on pedestals; understanding our human limitations is a great equalizer.

Knowing that all capable adults are responsible for themselves made my setting boundaries easier, too. Nor do I expect anyone else other than God to protect me or provide for my self-worth.

I grew up in a family where my anger wasn't okay—or emotions for that matter—and I learned to avoid them. My parents used explosive anger as discipline. Theirs was a painful and damaging laser. I learned to do whatever was necessary to make it go away. When others were angry, it made me uncomfortable because I felt responsible.

I learned the hard way how wrong I was, but it took a long time for me to realize I wasn't responsible for anyone else's poor choices. When my girls were little, their outbursts in the grocery or department store made me feel ashamed. Certain it was a reflection of my parenting, I'd try to get them to stop immediately, often yelling, "Stop it!" instead of addressing their real issues. Then I was full of guilt because I was using the same laser my parents had.

As a new believer, using the little I knew about God, I thought it seemed feasible to talk or pray my way out of anger. I said things like, "Compared to other husbands or children, mine are pretty good," or "In the scheme of eternity this isn't so bad." By avoiding the real issues, I could hide the laser, which enabled my husband and children to manipulate me, which stunted their character development.

Blinded to the truth by my experience and misconceptions, I needed God to break through my unhealthy thinking. Trying harder not to get mad wasn't the answer. Neither my husband nor I realized we had entered into this crazy dance in which he used his anger as a means of deflection and avoidance, and I moved with it. I'd remind him, for example, to take out the trash, and he'd overreact (out came his laser). Then I'd respond to his reaction (now I'm armed), and now we were both off the original topic of the trash (can you see the light sabers flashing?). The result is that I thought twice before ever bringing up the trash again. In truth, I simply figured it was easier to empty the trash myself than even to bring it up and risk another battle.

Once I recognized that I am not responsible for another person's reactions, I stopped helping my husband manipulate me. I see how unhealthy my thoughts were. I wasn't extending grace; instead I was enabling him to avoid the truth (he needed to take out the trash sometimes). Now I bring up issues regardless of how small I think they are, and if my husband overreacts, I wait. By refusing to be dragged into his tirade, I'm free to stick to the original topic. Once he's quiet, the topic can be restated. After a few weeks, my husband even noticed that he could no longer manipulate me.

For me, the amazing part about learning to address anger head-on is that it wasn't as painful as I thought it would be. Dealing with each issue took some hard work up front to get down to the bare truth. The irony is that my trying to avoid getting angry was, in fact, making me angrier. Staying in the arena of truth means I don't need to be angry. While anger is a laser used *incorrectly*, honesty guided by the hand of God is a powerful laser used *correctly*; it cuts and cauterizes a wound at the same time. Honesty doesn't leave the person torn and bleeding; it always prepares a person for healing, when they're ready.

Now I see that when honest communication is employed, both parties can come away empowered. This kind of honesty can remove the cancer of lies. Not flying off the handle preserved my dignity, even if I needed to change my perspective; not stuffing my feelings (then letting them ooze out later) brought closure. Even if the other person reacted poorly, I could walk away knowing I had done everything in my power to obtain a resolution, and that the way others responded was not my responsibility.

Finding and using my space, however, did not resolve everything in regard to my husband's betrayal. Changing my responses, for instance, was a lot easier than surrendering my anger. But as long as I saw myself as an innocent victim and my husband as the monster, pride was at the helm. The Enemy was there, of course, to whisper in my ear, continually reinforcing and fueling the lies. Pride and my perceived rights kept me tied to my pain and skewed my understanding of the situation.

But I have to know and focus on the truth. It's easy to keep thinking, "Why did my husband betray me like that? I have a right to be angry. I deserve to be treated better than this." In actuality, I don't want what I deserve because everyone deserves death. It's only because of God's grace and through Christ's sacrifice that life is even an option. According to God's standard, anything less perfect than He falls short of being satisfactory and is deserving of death. And from God's perspective, the consequences of death is eternal separation from God. When I took a hard look at my life, the only appropriate response was to tuck my pride away, get down on my knees, and then thank Jesus for saving my pitiful soul. My heart could hold just as much darkness as my husband's, and though I could judge good behavior from bad, I was not qualified to judge him.

The next step was to lay down my understanding of any situation. My view, after all, is based on personal experience, and is extremely limited compared to the perspective of God, who knows and sees everything. I've found it is wiser, then, to seek His perspective. Asking for help from Someone you can't physically see takes faith at first. Every time I did, God was faithful to shed His light into my condition and reveal His truth. It became easier to trust Him, and it became clear that when I ran ahead on my own, based on my own understanding, it always meant trouble.

God created each of us to carry our own load, but our burden shouldn't include more than one day's worth of anger. Our fury at first seems so sweet to embrace, but the longer we carry it, the more it becomes lumps of bitterness. As the lumps pile up, the Enemy manacles them to us with a chain of lies, turning us into the slaves of our burden. This bitterness has a pungent odor that others avoid while we remain oblivious to it. Our learning to deal with anger each day will ensure our lasting health and continued spiritual growth. We can learn to deal with anger by depending on Christ, whose golden glimmers of truth include the ones below.

- It's okay to be angry.
- I am not responsible for another's anger.
- I am responsible for my reactions (I make me mad).
- Anger should prompt prayerful self-examination.
- God is big enough to handle my anger.
- God is wise enough to lovingly show me the root of my bitterness.

Path Lights

GOD, slow to get angry and huge in loyal love,
  forgiving iniquity and rebellion and sin;
Still, never just whitewashing sin.
  But extending the fallout of parents' sins
to children into third,
  even the fourth generation.

(Num. 14:18)

The start of a quarrel is like a leak in a dam,
  so stop it before it bursts.

(Prov. 17:14)

A person without self-control
  is like a house with its doors and windows knocked out.

(Prov. 25:28)

Go head and be angry. You do well to be angry—but don't
use your anger as fuel for revenge. And don't stay angry.
Don't go to bed angry. Don't give the Devil that kind of foothold in your life. (Eph. 4:26–27)

God's righteousness doesn't grow from human anger. (James
1:20)

Journaling

Write about how your family members dealt with their anger and
what you learned about anger as a result. Think about people or situations that make you angry, and then pray for God to show you the
motive behind your anger. If anger is a problem for you, write out a
detailed plan describing how you'll make a space before reacting in
anger.

If you avoid anger at all cost, ask God to show you healthy ways
to deal with it. Picture the last time you were held back by another

person's anger, and ask God to show you a different way to respond. It's okay to tell another person that they do not have permission to yell at you or treat you poorly. When you speak up, you teach others how to treat you.

CHAPTER 6

Shadowlands

Avoiding Dark Places

We've all spent time in the shadows along the path on our journey to healing; places pocked by dark pits of pride—self-righteousness, resentments, and even self-reliance. We must take care to stay where the light is and go around the dark pits of pride that I call *shadowlands*. Our eyes must remain on Christ and our feet on the path that He has laid out. It's easy to mistake these pits as offering a cool place to retreat out of the sun, but they're really traps out of the Son's presence, and they are to be avoided.

As complicated in meaning as we sometimes make Scripture, its overriding theme is God's love. This love is not the human kind of affection, which is fickle. It is godly, completely selfless. This purest form of love from our Creator's heart is the perfect balance of mercy and justice. The depth of God's heart was glimpsed when His Son, Jesus, was on the cross, fully obedient to God's plan for His death. This kind of self-sacrifice looks like foolishness to a world born in sin and selfishness. Yet we were created for this type of love—we yearn for it, to both receive it and give it. Only God can pour this pure love into us, and we can't give it without His pouring; we can't produce it ourselves any more than a thistle can produce blackberries.

Humility in humans is the opposite of pride, and is the result of a person realizing that she is intimately known by God. When we see ourselves and others in the light of God's love, all is revealed and nothing is hidden. Who I am, who others are, who we all are in relation to God becomes clear. We are all His creation, made in His image, yet poor reflections. This is not news. But when I consider that God—the only One who has a right to be egotistical—took on humility by being willing to lay aside His glory for me, I am humbled. He accepted abject poverty after heaven to make a way for me to reach Him. Sin, the obstacle that separated me from God, had to be removed. Only innocent blood could wipe my sin out. Keeping this truth in perspective shines a new light on my own pride. When my eyes are on Christ, I want to live a life worthy of the price He paid.

My ego pulls me off course, depending on how much faith I place in myself. Being a pull-myself-up-by-the-bootstraps kind of gal, this happens a lot. Ego can be subtle. It whispers, "You should be in control of your life because faith in God is harder than faith in your own intellect." After I discovered my husband's betrayal, self-reliance and self-preservation were familiar shadowlands I often fell into. For a time, I felt as though God somehow didn't protect me or know me, so I dug in deeper.

Nothing holds a spirit hostage like the need to be in control. The saddest part is that this need is a self-made pit. Every time my goal consisted of being in control, I left God out of the decision making and shut off His power. My pit was full of reasons why I was right and others were wrong, and why they didn't deserve forgiveness. As less light of truth got in, the deeper I dug myself into the pit of pride.

To do any digging, a person needs a shovel—and emotions serve as the shovel. Not all emotions are unfounded, of course. Feeling grief after a significant loss is perfectly legitimate. Grief that results from betrayal, though, can be tricky. I had to ask myself, "Am I grieving over loss of trust and security? Or am I grieving because this just isn't fair and I deserve better than this?"

Emotions keep us in the pit, and any emotion not founded in God's truth is the shovel we use to dig ourselves in deeper. While my emotions feel real to me, they aren't the real problem I must deal with. God created feelings as indicators of spiritual well-being. Fear, resentment, and worry should have been my indicators that I was in a pit. Instead, I often assumed they should guide my decisions, so I acted rashly, and ended up camping out in the pit with my shovel.

Rather, these emotional indicators should have encouraged me to pray and seek God's wisdom. Any emotion has the potential to keep me in a self-centered pit, but when I chose instead to let them guide me to a place of prayer, I was given illumination and I could see my way out of the pit. Whether I stayed in the pit or climbed out always depended on how I dealt with the emotions and the driving force of those emotions. But each time I fell into the pit, I needed to ask God to shine His light of truth into it to show me the way out. But first I had to put the shovel down and stop digging.

Our desire to lean on our own intellect is understandable. Intellect develops from past experience and we use it to discover much of what is true. Not wanting to look stupid, I tried hard to learn from past mistakes and my environment. In an attempt to reduce pain, I picked up unhealthy coping strategies in the process. But God also wants to use experiences to teach us. Faith is trusting God's character, even when the evidence suggests doing the opposite. When I accepted Christ as my Savior, my old method of learning had to become new. I recognized that He is the only thing worthy of my reliance. He was and is all I need. I had to replace my own attempts to change myself with Christ Himself. He was able to do the work I alone never could.

I know that trusting what we can't see feels risky and illogical at first, like putting faith in an inanimate object. I remember my first steps of faith, but experience soon revealed that God was trustworthy and real. My trust in Him grew. When I compared that to the darkness of trying on my own to no avail, I soon realized that it was not foolishness to place faith in an all-powerful God; it was foolishness to place faith in myself.

Tammy, by placing her faith in God, was growing stronger every day. Although she knew she could count on Christ, Tammy prayed for a person to talk with. She wasn't ready to try another group, and any extra money was going into her savings account for the future, so a counselor would have to wait.

I was really amazed when I received a call from one of the ladies in the Bible study. She was so sweet.

"I noticed you hadn't come back to our group and I don't blame you" she said. "After the way you were put on the spot, I decided to call it quits too. I felt a need to call you. I'm not sure why, but some of the things you said about your marriage resonated with me."

She told me that her husband was a pilot and was gone a lot, and that she felt isolated. I knew what was coming. My heart was pounding like crazy as the Holy Spirit led me to ask a question.

"Do you think it's possible that your husband has been unfaithful?" As soon as the word "unfaithful" came out, she started to cry. We both knew Who was behind this call, and the answer to both of our prayers. "Thanks, Lord."

We met for coffee and talked for nearly three hours. It was good to have someone who really understood my emotions. What surprised me was learning how far I'd come. I remembered my old self, who felt powerless. That old self was now sitting across the table from me in this woman. Being able to encourage her gave me more strength and made me feel even more hopeful.

I have no doubt that I can go wherever God leads, and if my husband doesn't start working on his own healing, then I'll have to file for divorce. My new friend and I are both praying for what God wants.

The next time I saw my husband, I told him what I needed. I said if he wanted me to consider reconciliation, he'd need to start seeing a counselor, go to church, find a Christian man or small group to be accountable to, and he needed to grow spiritually.

I braced myself for an argument, but he picked up his

phone and called a counselor. I was shocked. He said he
didn't like being alone, and he missed his family. It took all
my strength not to say, "You should have thought of that
before." Instead I asked him how he'd pay for counseling.
He said his medical insurance would pay for it. Thank You,
God.

⚭

As Stephanie pushed through her fear of being out of control and
handing it over to God, she soon had a "lighter" feeling. She was
more hopeful—and it had nothing to do with her husband. His behavior hadn't really changed, but hers had.

I'm not sure if there are words to describe the freedom I'm
feeling. My not having all the answers hasn't brought the
world to an end. It's actually refreshing not having to be
everything to everyone. In the past, I would have proudly
described myself as self-sufficient and independent. Now
I see that I'm *in*sufficient on my own. I need to be God-
dependant, because that's where real power is. No more
posing as the one who has it all together. I'm just beginning
to realize how exhausting it was.

My group has become the highlight of my week. I go there
for my "truth fix." It seems so ironic to me; God is such a
paradox—that I gain such freedom by being dependent. I'm
someone who always wants things to be logical, so accepting that such a paradox is true is a real challenge. Of course
freedom through dependence now makes sense, because if I
could figure everything out on my own, what would I need
Jesus for? As it is, I need Him and can trust Him for every
little thing.

When my mind begins to ask all the old questions, and
I wonder when my husband will change, I simply pray. I
find peace when I place everything—from my work to my
husband—at the foot of the cross. Jesus is absolutely faithful.

He will never leave me alone; He'll guide me one day at a time. At this point I don't even know where my marriage fits into His plan, but I know He will guide me about that, too. Until then, I will continue to pray for my husband and trust in God while I wait to see how it all turns out.

Given the nature of the sites my husband was on, and knowing more about this addiction, I felt God saying it's time to get tested for STDs. I could no longer put my health and life on the altar of my husband's selfishness. I was terrified but had to know the truth.

◌

Renee and her husband have been moving closer, little by little, and by learning what humility really means, she's been enjoying the freedom from explosive anger.

I've been on several dates with my husband, and I'm beginning to have more hope. The boys are too. They're spending more time on the phone with their dad, and they're really glad that he's coming to their sporting events. When he came to the house for dinner, it felt like old times.

I'm really encouraged by the way we've been able to share what's in our hearts and what God has been showing us. In the last couple of months, my husband has opened up more about his childhood and past hurts, more than he had in all the years I've known him. He even gave me spiritual input about *my* life. But old habits die hard, and instead of thanking God for my husband's spiritual growth, his comments stirred the old anger pot.

When I talked to my counselor, she asked me who really was the leader of our home. As I thought about it, I got it. I took the lead, and now my husband was stepping on my toes. The real kicker is, I'd been praying for him to step up for years.

Pride can cause anger and quick decisions that are based more in emotion than on truth. Pride expressed as a selfish attitude can also keep women from taking healthy steps, even when it's way past time for her to move on without her husband. Her fearful emotions—over losing the image of the happy family, over losing income and prestige, over admitting imperfections—hinder her from trusting God. Some women have even quoted Scripture to me, like "God hates divorce." Though this is true, God also hates sin. The greater truth is that He doesn't hate *sinners* or divorced *people*. His plan for a person's life is never thwarted because of a bad choice—theirs or someone else's. He is bigger than sin and its consequences—He is the only cure for it.

Tammy had to lay down her pride and allow herself to be vulnerable with another person. She was wise to pray and wait for God to bring the right person, who turned out to be an encouragement to her. She found someone safe to talk to and a partner to walk the road to healing with, both of them knowing that God had made the connection. God is not a God of confusion. Patience and waiting for His answer and direction brought them both one step closer to healing.

Stephanie found the freedom that comes when we stop trying to figure everything out on our own. She's allowing God to speak through her group and is growing in Christ.

Faith will always be the opposite of sight, and fear usually follows when God asks us to step into the unknown—but He walks with us every time. He also only illuminates one step at a time. As much as we'd love a complete road map, He knows we'd turn our focus from Him and onto the map.

Renee is finding a new pit of pride in being the spiritual head of the household. Her faith had always been greater than her husband's, and the boys looked to her when it came to spiritual issues. She thought she wanted her husband to step up, but once he started making headway, her resentment surfaced. This made her realize she had a sore spot when it came to his taking the lead. She had more work to do.

When God humbles us, it's never easy on us. I remember thinking that it made sense to cut my losses and run. I didn't want to be the fool again. This felt like a rational decision, and I could have backed it with Scripture. God made it clear to me through the Holy Spirit, however, that I was not free to leave my marriage. There was no peace in that decision. God, being omniscient, knew there was still hope. Though it wasn't what I wanted to hear, I listened. In my spirit His assurance resonated: God wasn't calling me to a life of heart-wrenching pain and being physically at risk over and over. If my husband chose to go back to his old life, I would then be free to go.

I'm glad I listened to God and took another chance. Had I trusted in, and acted on, my own logic and pride, I would have missed out on so much healing. I would also most likely be married to a whole new set of problems—or the same ones in a new set of clothes. God understood my need to get healthy first. I trusted His heart of love for me.

We have to be careful not to grab onto one piece of the truth while missing the whole intent. God's heart is for His creation, and as His children we have available all the resources of heaven if we will reach out in faith. I have never seen anyone put total trust in God and be disappointed—never. I have, however, seen many people ask God to bless their plans, then go ahead with less than perfect results.

Giving up is not the same as surrendering, any more than breaking is the same as bending. When we surrender to God, we will hand over our right to self out of a heart of trust, not a crushed spirit. We honor God when we seek His best and acknowledge His sovereignty. He is a gentleman waiting for us to bow so He can come in and reign. This pliability is a picture of true humility. Pride is what keeps us rigid and unable to bend.

Pride doesn't always express itself as selfishness or arrogance. It can also disguise itself as false humility or self-deprecation. For example, I would say, "It isn't that I don't trust God, but I don't trust myself to trust Him." I was hung up by what I couldn't do, and I'd beat myself up every time I failed. "I" was at the center, and it was all about me. The harder I tried to please God, the more I failed. I was unworthy of God. Knowing I could never be worthy of Christ's love, I assumed I was worthless—and the Enemy confirmed it.

Then I learned the truth. When my focus was on my failure, or even on my success, I was expressing pride. Either way, I am not worthy. But being unworthy is not the same thing as being worthless. My value, in fact, comes from my Creator—God Almighty.

We have value because of the One who created us. We're all like priceless works of art. The value of a painting, for example, has nothing to do with the type of paint or canvas used. Its value comes from the artist who created it. When produced by a master, a painting's worth is almost incalculable. Since the Ultimate Master created us all, our worth is immeasurable. So in doubting myself, I doubted God. This realization changed the way I saw myself. As I surrendered fully to God's plan, there was nothing Christ couldn't do in me and through me. I got out of the way.

I often see other women who have gone deeper into a pit. Settling in the dark, their pride is expressed in being a victim, sure that they can't come out. This is a common pit in the shadowland. There, women can find identity and sympathy. Finding others who will say, "That's terrible and unfair," or "You poor thing," keeps these women dwelling in their pits, feeling safe because their pride is based on pointing out what others have done. It keeps the focus off what they need to do as well as what God wants them to do. They don't see the arrogance in deciding that their situations are somehow too big for even God.

These decisions never take God by surprise. Living in a broken world where people have free will means we each hold the power to hurt others and ourselves. Just because God doesn't stop an evil act doesn't mean that He planned it. He has put His overriding plan of hope and healing in place for all of His children. Though He doesn't remove the pain we face, He walks through it with us, providing the strength, wisdom, and power we lack on our own. He knew we'd end up in some dark places; that's why He is the Light of the World. When we remain a victim, our fear keeps us from using our best resource—Christ—the One who knows better than anyone the pain of betrayal and abuse—and who is the only way out.

Telling a victim's tale was once a dark, lonely pit for me. I'd set myself up as judge and jury of my husband. I've since learned that I have no power or responsibility to change someone else, and it's a full-time job working just on me. Any focus aimed at blaming, changing, or judging others is wasted energy better spent on myself. Since God will use the standard on me that I use on others, I'd be better off to have Him find me extending large measures of grace to others, so that I'll be judged by the same measure when my judgment comes.

This doesn't mean I ignore others, or worse, make excuses for them. We need to strike a balance. I have a responsibility to be discerning about behaviors, to set boundaries, and to hold others accountable for their actions. But these are not the same as a value judgment of the whole person or that person's heart. Boundaries come from a healthy understanding of every person's intrinsic value, but those boundaries should be based on truth and love—never pride.

Writing someone off as worthy of my judgment is prideful. It's another way we try to be God. There's a fine line between loving the sinner while hating the sin. It can only be found with the Holy Spirit's help. I'm finding that there is so much power available to me when I surrender any right to exact judgment, pray, and then wait for God's answer about how best to deal with the other person. Only God can know that person's heart, so it is best that I wait for Him to reveal my next step.

The shadowlands of pride lie all around us on the path to healing. They can at first appear to be just a shady spot to sit and rest, and without some divine help, we aren't even able to recognize it as a pit. I used to pray for God to help me in the obvious areas of struggle— those I inherited from my family of origin and other challenges I picked up along the side roads of life. I still pray for His help in these areas. But after walking with hundreds of hurting women, I now pray more fervently for God to reveal the hard-to-detect shadow- lands in my life—those dark pits that others can see, though I'm blind to them. Those are the places where I can do the most damage and the most damage can be done to me.

God has been faithful to shine His light into many of these dark places, and I'm grateful—though every time He does, my climbing out is painful. It's much like lancing a boil or cleaning a wound; in being freed from the pit, the healing process is accelerated, but there's a cost in ridding myself of false pride. I used to wonder when "arrival" happens. I now see we don't arrive until we go home to the Lord. The good news is, the character work I allow God to do in me will accompany me into eternity.

There's hard work in surrendering to God. Being a follower of Christ is all about getting to know the heart of God and having a close relationship. The best part is, this relationship is the only one we take into heaven. So I must choose to get to know Jesus. If I don't, the end of my life could look like this: I walk slowly up to the pearly gates and wait while someone checks to see if my name is in the book. I then walk forward to shake Jesus' hand, but I walk slowly because I don't know Him that well.

For me, getting to know Him better means that I'll run through the pearly gates, jump into my Lord's lap, give Him a big hug, and finish the conversation we started that morning.

Here are more glimmers for those who want to run:

- I don't always get to know why.
- Surrendering to God is not the same as giving up.
- Truth sometimes comes with pain.
- God is big enough to handle anything.
- God will lovingly reveal my shadowlands.

Path Lights

Dear friend, listen well to my words;
    tune your ears to my voice.
Keep my message in plain view at all times.
    Concentrate! Learn it by heart!
Those who discover these words live, really live;
    body and soul, they're bursting with health.
                  (Prov. 4:20–22)

Let the peace of Christ keep you in tune with each other, in step with each other. None of this going off and doing your own thing. And cultivate thankfulness. Let the Word of Christ—the Message—have the run of the house. (Col. 3:15–16)

At the time, discipline isn't much fun. It always feels like it's going against the grain. Later, of course, it pays off handsomely, for it's the well-trained who find themselves mature in their relationship with God. (Heb. 12:11)

But friends, that's exactly who we are: children of God. And that's only the beginning. Who knows how we'll end up! What we know is that when Christ is openly revealed, we'll see him—and in seeing him, become like him. (1 John 3:2)

God is love. When we take up permanent residence in a life of love, we live in God and God lives in us. This way, love has the run of the house, becomes at home and mature in us, so that we're free of worry on Judgment Day. (1 John 4:16–17)

Journaling

In your journal, write down some of the areas that you and God agree need work. Pray and ask Him to show you specifically what needs to be done in those areas. Then pray for His insight into those shadowlands yet undiscovered. Tell Him if you are willing to do what needs doing, and He'll do the rest. As you wait for His direction, be sure to write down what He reveals.

CHAPTER 7

Glowworms

Absorbing and Applying Grace

I can count on one hand the number of people I know who have "it." "It" is hard to define, but people who have "it" seem to radiate care and to value everyone who gets near them. For years I couldn't figure out what drew me to these people. I now understand that "it" was grace—God's grace, like the soft luminescence of a *glowworm*. Grace is undeserved favor and unconditional love. Others are irresistibly drawn to a person who has Christ emanating through her. This person allows the Holy Spirit to fill her with warmth until her glow shines all around her.

Glowworms must first fully accept God's grace into their own lives. But once people are filled by this gift of grace that they can never earn, they naturally pour it out onto others. Grace flows out of the heart—a heart full of thanksgiving and humility. Once people find the stream of Living Water, they want others—everyone—to experience it. This desire is in stark contrast to codependency, a condition in which a person gives and gives out of her need or emptiness, hoping to be filled in return. Resentment and exhaustion are the typical results.

When, at fifteen, I became a Christian, I didn't have a full understanding of what growing in Christ looked like. I knew that my decision to accept Christ as my Savior meant that all my sins were forgiven and that, after my physical death, I would spend eternity in heaven. I understood in my head what the gift and my decision meant. So over the years I worked hard to be a good person. Out of gratitude for what Christ had done, I trudged through the Bible, looking for answers, and did all the things I thought good Christians did: I went to church, Bible studies, retreats, and conferences. I failed a lot. My intentions were good, but my heart couldn't produce the "it" that only God could provide.

Years went by before I began to fully understand *grace*, and that's when I began to see change in myself. In the first chapter of this book, I ended my story with my asking God, "Why me?" But my questions didn't stop there. After more crying out to God with "Why?" my husband and I cried and talked, and cried again.

When the last few details of Dave's story finally came out, in that darkest moment, God revealed His grace in the most personal and intimate way. I remember looking down at my husband slumped on the floor in shame. That small voice, like a whisper, comforted me— and then God gave me a glimpse of how He saw Dave. That shift in perspective let me see for the first time that my husband was not a monster, but a little boy carrying around thirty years of pain.

Then God gently and lovingly answered my "Why?" I heard His voice in my head as clearly as if He had spoken out loud. He said, "If you don't extend My grace to Dave now, he may never know it." I was humbled and broken. I saw the pride behind my *Whys?*—as if God owed me some explanation. God didn't owe me anything. But He had given me a choice. God put Dave and I together for this moment. I looked at Dave crumpled on the floor by the bed as he wept uncontrollably, and with a strength that was not my own, I put my arm around him.

Instantly something broke loose spiritually. We both could almost hear the chains rattle as they fell to the floor. My husband later shared how significant that moment was for him. It was the beginning of the healing process for both of us.

When in that moment God asked me to extend grace to my husband, all the years of study and my desire to be like Christ were tested. In the midst of emotional pain, after days of crying out to Him, I heard God's gentle voice tell me that it all came down to a choice. Would I extend the grace that God had given to me? Then the responsibility of that choice hit me. Dave might never know God's grace if I didn't extend it to him. God had allowed me to be in this place for such a time as this.

In that moment, the shift in my perspective revealed a whole new vista. All the knowledge I'd accumulated about who God is—His justice and mercy, His grace and what it cost Him—became real and personal. I stood there at a fork in the path, before me two ways clearly delineated, and was moved from the "head choice" I'd made at age fifteen into a "heart choice." Instead of letting my pain and emotion do the talking, instead of saying why I felt justified in condemning my husband, I stepped aside and let God determine my actions. Though a hug went against everything in me, the moment I obeyed and acted, God's glory was evident. Both Dave and I changed.

God's grace is the opposite of judgment—it is undeserved. And our offering is our chance to let God do through us what we could never do alone. This is not some religious concept; it is gut wrenching, soul reaching, life changing—*grace.*

Soft-spoken Tammy had found her voice. She was encouraged by her husband's first steps, but she needed to see some consistency over time before she'd be satisfied that he was serious about getting help and doing the hard work of recovery. Dealing with her own issues was first priority. She was thankful for the books she'd read, the prayer partner God had provided, and the Bible.

> My prayer times have been a blessing. It's been good to get another person's perspective. I've noticed that my woman friend seems to have misplaced her anger on the adult entertainment industry. It would have been easy to join her there, but God led me to ask her some questions instead.
>
> "You do realize that many of those women are also vic-

tims? They didn't wake up and decide they wanted to turn tricks or do adult films."

"Give me a break," she said. "They could find work in a million other places. None of the people involved in the sex industry care anything about the marriages and families being destroyed. Every message they make seems to be about controlling men by their shorts. And it's not just the adult entertainment industry. Look at the way young women— and even young *girls*—dress these days!"

She was pretty worked up, so I dropped it. God had provided a lamp for me to see my pitfalls. I'm glad that we're reading together, and I trust God to deal with our anger in His time. I was in the same place not too long ago. Then God showed me the pain it took for women to get to the place where they're willing to sell their bodies and souls; but for the grace of God, it could be me. My need to pass judgment began to dissolve as I saw so many of us buy the lie that our self-worth is tied to our sexuality and how attractive we are.

My husband seemed serious about getting help. I could see how hard it was for him. When he called after his last counseling appointment, he sounded like he'd been to war. I guess he had—a spiritual war.

Stephanie continued to look for balance between relying on her logical self and trusting in God. She'd been determined to be superwife and stick with her husband to the end, but then she received a huge wake-up call.

I was cleaning out my office on a Saturday, trying not to dive into work. My husband was out playing tennis. Then the phone rang, and I was surprised to hear my doctor's voice. She explained that she often caught up on phone calls on Saturdays—then she said the results of my blood work were in. My throat went dry as I waited for the rest of the news. It was bad. The STD I had contracted was not life threatening, but I needed to get started on antibiotics right away, and she would phone in the prescription. She also wanted to see me first thing Monday morning to go over everything in detail, and my husband should also be tested. It was all professional, cut and dried. All my false hope and denial were gone.

I wasn't angry, to my surprise, as I was when I discovered the betrayal. This was more like an answer to a question I'd been afraid to ask. I sensed God was giving me the power to let go and stop fighting. He had the answer and had prepared me to see the truth. A wave of sadness came over me as I finally started to grieve the loss.

I told my group, but they simply asked me what I felt God leading me to do. I told them that His plan was unfolding— that I'd shifted gears out of fixing my husband and into letting God fix me. I was putting my finances in order and preparing for my husband's poor response. I knew enough not to make an actual move without a divine confirmation. I couldn't let the old "take-charge" Stephanie move back in now. I still had praying, mourning, and planning to do.

○)

Renee was beginning to believe that she and her husband might be able to reconcile and start over. Then she hit another bump in the road.

I was giddy! I thought that my family could be put back to-gether. I was just about to ask my husband to move back in—then he dropped the news in my lap.

"Renee . . . I don't want to go backward, because we seem to be moving ahead so well. But my counselor says that I can't have any secrets."

"What is it?" I wasn't ready for what he said next.

"I had another affair . . . years ago . . . when we were first married. I know now that it was all part of my need for validation; it was a way to cope. That doesn't excuse the pain I've caused you, and I've prayed that it won't unravel the progress we've made so far."

I couldn't talk or even breathe. It was like a second punch in the gut. Of course I was angry. Flaming mad at God. Why would He get my hopes up only to dash them? But this time the volcano didn't erupt. I left quickly and went home to process this new pain. The boys met me at the door as I rushed in.

"Mom, what's wrong? You look like you've seen an accident. Is Dad okay?"

Is Dad *okay?* I wanted to explode, but I could actually feel myself resisting the habit of putting my pride first. I knew to choose my words carefully. "Guys . . . I need you to pray. Your dad is fine. I can't talk right now, because I need a few minutes to get my head straight."

Oh . . . how I fought the old voices; I wanted to just let my anger blow. Thankfully, I felt divine intervention. This news was going to be hard enough on my sons without their mother spewing it out on top of her rage. "Oh God, how will we survive yet another blow?"

Grace is something a human heart cannot produce. We simply choose to let God pour it in and through us—or not. When we're filled with the Spirit, the glow of grace, much like a glowworm's bioluminescence, is evident. When it comes to grace, Christ is not only our example of grace, He is the source. The hard part is being obedient and trusting in the truth when the Enemy is trying to fill us with all the reasons that our anger is justified. When grace dwells in us, we look different and then make a difference. Grace changed the way Renee reacted to her husband's confession because she trusted God to give her a new perspective.

There's one more detail. Grace isn't *grace* when it costs us nothing.

If I decide to simply let someone off the hook and God isn't in it, then I'm a doormat or enabler (someone who allows another to remain unhealthy by removing accountability). Stephanie was beginning to realize that remaining in the house with her husband would be a silent endorsement of his behavior, and resuming sex with him could cost her life. Grace doesn't remove the consequences of a poor choice—it removes the need to condemn. Offering counterfeit grace is a common mistake that women in the church make. They're not looking at an offender the way God does; they are taking the path of least resistance, or avoiding confrontation, or hoping the offender will be sorry enough not ever to offend again. All the hopes and good intentions in the world do not equal one ounce of *grace*. It's up to God to decide when and where we serve and sacrifice. Grace means God decides—and I obey.

Some time after discovering my husband's betrayal, I attended a county fair. It was a warm summer day, and there were many provocatively dressed women in the crowd. Much like Tammy's friend, I stopped seeing people and saw temptresses instead. Anger and indignation rose within me by the minute. Then I stood face-to-face with a woman selling ice cream. Her blouse was revealing, to say the least, and her face was covered with too much makeup. Before I could formulate a nasty thought, I heard a gentle thought in my mind, which could not have come from my heart of condemnation. It said, "Consider what this woman has gone through in her life that created her need to draw attention to herself. Could it be that she's a victim instead of the enemy? Isn't it time to lay down your indignation and extend her My grace?"

Only God could give me His heart for women who are in the sex industry, for women who dress seductively, and for young women all over the world. They are often abused, addicted, and discarded. Their behavior stems from their own pain and didn't develop overnight. No self-respecting woman would choose to be objectified, degraded, and used.

If you're hearing this defense for the first time, and your pain is fresh and raw, don't expect to accept it right away. It takes time to catch your breath and sift through all the layers of pain. No one expects you to jump right into grace and forgiveness. Renee couldn't jump from rage to grace, yet Christ is guiding her there. Read with the hope and assurance that God can get you there in His time. Meanwhile, give *yourself* grace.

I tried for years to muster up Christlikeness and extend grace. No one was fooled except me. What I thought was grace was a cheap counterfeit. Good behavior could never substitute for being surrendered to, and guided by, God's Holy Spirit. Christ wants to live through me, not be misrepresented by me. I give thanks for His ubiquitous patience with me and for showing me the truth: all my striving was the opposite of surrendering and was hard work expended for no return.

I still pray for God to give me a heart of compassion for all of His hurting children. Daily I give thanks for His patience with me and His unfailing love. I pray for more of His heart of *grace*. I have seen the difference the Holy Spirit makes time and time again, and yet even with all of these sightings, I'm convinced that what I've seen is only a glimmer of what He has to offer. Hear are more glimmers to add to your collection.

- I can't, but God can.
- God loves me.
- God can change what I can't.
- His grace is enough.
- Grace casts a light that changes everything.

Path Lights

Above all and before all, do this: Get Wisdom!
Write this at the top of your list: Get Understanding!
(Prov. 4:7)

GOD, order a peaceful and whole life for us
because everything we've done, you've done for us.
(Isa. 26:12)

Are you tired? Worn out? Burned out on religion? Come to me. Get away with me and you'll recover your life. I'll show you how to take a real rest. Walk with me and work with me—watch how I do it. Learn the unforced rhythms of grace. (Matt. 11:28–29)

Sin can't tell you how to live. After all, you're not living under that old tyranny any longer. You're living in the freedom of God. (Rom. 6:14)

Is it not clear to you that to go back to that old rule-keeping, peer-pleasing religion would be an abandonment of everything personal and free in my relationship with God? I refuse to do that, to repudiate God's grace. If a living relationship with God could come by rule-keeping, then Christ died unnecessarily. (Gal. 2:21)

Saving is all his idea, and all his work. All we do is trust him enough to let him do it. It's God's gift from start to finish! We don't play the major role. If we did, we'd probably go around bragging that we'd done the whole thing! (Eph. 2:8–9)

Journaling

Write a thank-you note to God for His amazing grace. Pray, and ask Him to fill you up with His love and show you the ways He has gently guided you to this place. Take any hard places where forgiveness won't grow and lay them at the feet of Christ. Picture His understanding smile as He looks at you with love, not condemnation. Write a description or draw a picture of what grace looks like. Be filled up each day, and then spill grace on everyone you meet.

CHAPTER 8

Firefly

The Glowworm with Wings

The glowworm is not the only insect to produce its own light. If you take a glowworm and give it wings, it's called a *firefly*. If you take grace and give it wings, it's called forgiveness—and it is forgiveness that takes God's grace to the sky. In the same way that wings offer the firefly freedom from gravity, forgiveness equals freedom to us. Imagine the feel of soaring over a grassy knoll after being limited to crawling on a few blades.

Forgiveness is one of the most misunderstood of religious concepts. Too many Christians try to offer a weak substitute that lacks the power of the real thing. The freedom that comes with forgiveness is a powerful gift, but it must be entered into with caution—it comes with responsibility. Forgiveness is not easy. When I extend forgiveness, I'm agreeing to live with the consequences of another's poor choice—and I must also give up my right to punish. The other extreme is enabling, protecting a person from the natural consequences of his or her choices, stalling that person's growth.

Forgiveness doesn't mean that what the other person did was okay, nor is it letting that person off the hook. It must be understood that the person's value doesn't change because of a poor choice.

Forgiveness, too, is a choice not a feeling. If, for example, I wait until my feelings soften toward an offender, it would take me forever to forgive him or her. Once I decide to forgive, however, the feelings follow. If the offender continues in unhealthy behavior, my forgiving that person doesn't have to mean that I must maintain a friendship with him or her, or stay in contact with that person. It does mean that if I walk away, I know I did all I could to help the offender learn, grow, and change. I've left behind a glimmer of hope, but that person's changing is all up to him or her.

Forget about the old saying, "Forgive and forget." If we could forget, we wouldn't need to forgive. Rather, when our injuries are great, we need to process through layers of forgiveness. I agreed in the beginning to enter into the forgiveness *process* with my husband. I made progress through the first layer, so when a new layer appeared, I could process through it separately without feeling like I hadn't really forgiven him at all.

It would have been too simplistic to say, "I forgive my husband for all his poor choices." I needed time to process through all the consequences I was agreeing to live with. The first layer was forgiving him for the pain of the overall betrayal, but additional layers were uncovered that had to be sifted through. Emotional, spiritual, financial, and family issues are just a few of those layers. It took time for me to realize how many layers there were and how each area had been affected.

Many months after the final discovery of Dave's full activities, I felt as if we'd sifted through most of the layers of forgiveness. Then the topic of money came up on an unrelated issue. Resentment crashed down on me like a giant redwood. It hit me hard that, for all those years, we'd been pinching pennies while my husband was spending money on his addiction. I had to step back and process where the strong emotion was coming from. I realized this was a layer I hadn't yet dealt with. I had to work through forgiveness again before we could move forward.

My husband knows I'm committed to forgiveness when he sees me process through every stage without condemnation. I'm honest about the pain a particular layer causes me, because it's a consequence of his poor choices. I don't throw it in his face or use it as a weapon since I want to rebuild the relationship, not tear it down. At first I went too far the other way, trying to hide the pain because I didn't want to push him back into his addiction. Then I realized this was unhealthy for both of us. He needed to know how I was feeling, and when he handled it without being defensive, we both moved forward in rebuilding trust.

It's important to recognize that forgiveness is not the same as trust, though they're closely tied and are simultaneous processes. Trust takes longer to rebuild. So many husbands want their wives to "get over it" and are frustrated by their wives' lack of trust. These husbands feel that they have to account for everything they do or say. Accountability is essential to rebuilding trust and is a consequence of poor choices. Never feel pressure to trust before you're ready—but always believe his behaviors. An innocent man should have no qualms about submitting to accountability or scrutiny, especially if he desires to regain trust.

Of course, this doesn't mean that you become his warden, either. His primary accountability should be to another man, or group of men, whom your husband is in contact with on a regular basis. A husband's submitting to a counselor, pastor, or men's group who will ask the hard questions is evidence of growth. A man committed to healing should grow spiritually from Bible study, reading, and prayer. Where appropriate, computer monitoring, filtering, and financial controls should be in place. The amount of resistance a husband puts up to accountability says a lot about how serious he is in his desire to heal. Remember—believe his behaviors.

Tammy continued to meet with her prayer partner, but she noticed some tension between them as their paths seemed to go in different directions.

I was so excited! And I wanted to share with my friend the latest breakthrough with my husband. From the moment we sat down, there was heaviness in the air. I decided it was best to first ask how she was doing. Our entire time together became one long complaint. Her husband wasn't doing enough. Her kids were acting out at her and each other. She felt angry all the time.

I tried to drop little suggestions and words of encouragement, but they bounced off her like a rubber ball off a brick wall. Nothing I said seemed to help. I asked her if she was seeing a counselor, which only led to another fifteen minutes of financial woes.

I walked away with a headache, and I felt drained and wrung out. I prayed for God to give me wisdom and to give my friend a new perspective. I wanted to speak the truth, but without coming across like I had all the answers. I wish she could see that she was really wallowing in her current pain and was just making it worse. I'm already dreading our next meeting.

After meeting with her doctor, Stephanie was thankful that the women in her group handled it without any judgment. She thanked God the STD was treatable, and then she prayed for strength to do what God was calling her to do.

I don't know if I can put into words what it feels like. The man I've given my life to put his addiction before my health and life. It was as if he'd put a gun to my head in a game of Russian roulette. To make matters worse, he has no clue how I feel, or any remorse over his choices.

This new information about the STD has brought a deeper sense of loss, but also a great deal of clarity. It's as if a haze has lifted, and I can see my circumstances with new eyes. God is all I need. He is the One holding the pilot's wheel at this point since I now know my compass is broken. I can trust Him to guide me. My finances are in order, my assets secure. The credit cards are all paid, and are either in his name or mine, but not joint. I've found an apartment and a lawyer.

My feelings range from anger to sadness. I even feel pockets of peace as I reflect on all that God has done so far. He is giving me His strength and wisdom. I thank Him daily for His provision and will trust Him with the future. I know He will guide the process of confronting my husband with my decision to divorce. My pastor will be with me, and so will my Lord.

As for my husband, I pray this will be hitting bottom for him and that he'll find the motivation to seek the healing available in Christ. It will take time for me to forgive— the wound is too deep. Even if he were to ask me to stay, I couldn't. Much would have to change before I could feel safe, so I'll have to watch from a distance. Either way, I'm fine—safe with Christ.

Renee was still reeling from her husband's latest confession.

I felt myself fighting to go back to the old angry place. My rage was calling to me, saying, "Go ahead! Explode! You'll feel better!" Thankfully, the healthy part of me, and God's Spirit, was stronger. The Lord wouldn't let me go. Each time I was alone with Christ, His encouragement kept me focused on His truth.

Lines of dialogue ran through my head like ticker tape: "Look at you. Well done! You didn't fly into that old rage"; "Don't let this new information erase all of the good work already done." Then the kicker, "Your husband took a huge risk being honest—now that things were looking up." The last bit of rage drained away and I picked up the phone.

I could tell by my husband's voice that he wasn't sure what I'd say. I asked if we could meet for lunch, and he agreed, but he asked, "Should I wear armor?" I laughed and added, "I guess I can't blame you for asking." The humor eased the tension and I began to really look forward to our meeting, I decided to wear an outfit that's one of his favorites. I even caught myself humming.

The lunch went well, but not perfect. We couldn't agree on what or when to tell the boys. My husband wasn't sure why they should be hurt again. I assumed he was protecting himself. So I suggested we both pray about it, and talk to someone who's further along in this process. Our lunch wasn't the love fest I'd hoped for, but it was another step forward.

I still had some work to do in the area of trust. I'd forgiven my husband, but trust would take much longer to rebuild. We'd both have to work on that, one new reaction at a time. It would also take time for him to stop expecting the old Renee to show up in a rage.

❧

Tammy's friend was carrying around the toxic waste of unforgiveness and resentment, and she splashed it on Tammy at their last meeting. She seemed to grow continually bitter with every perceived infraction. Stuck in the pit, she daily dug it deeper, adding new justifications. She couldn't see that the depth of her pit was interfering with her friendship with Tammy.

Tammy, on the other hand, continued giving her pride and anger to God. Even after this new, deep wound from her prayer partner, Tammy, instead of crawling into the pit with her, chose to trust Christ. Choosing not to get bogged down by the responses of others, she let the disappointment of her situation motivate her to take care of herself.

It made an amazing difference when Renee took a step back from her husband's recent confession. By not allowing her rage to fuel the fire, she enabled God's Spirit to minister to her with truth. No one said she didn't have a right to be angry, or that she should just forget what happened. She was, however, able to see the situation from another angle and enter into the forgiveness process.

Forgiveness is never easy, made harder when the offender shows little or no remorse. It would seem to make sense to wait for an offending husband to ask for forgiveness. But that puts him in the driver's seat, effectively letting him decide when and if the wife ever moves forward. A wife's decision to heal should have nothing to do with her husband's understanding of what he has done.

The best reason to forgive is because Christ asks me to, and because He forgave me first. If I've accepted the forgiveness offered on the cross at the exorbitant price of His life, then how can I balk at giving so much less? The story of the ungrateful servant, found in Matthew 18:21–35, makes it clear to me what God wants, and how He sees me when I refuse to forgive someone else.

I never want to give the impression that forgiveness is easy or should be easy. Holding on to the pain, though, and staying chained to past events is, in the long run, much harder. It not only takes more energy, it verifies the lies of the Enemy. One lie says, "If I hold onto this anger for a good long time, then my husband will 'get' what he's done." Another says, "If I forgive him, then he gets off scot-free." Or, "I need to hold onto my right to punish him with my anger."

There are many variations to the above lies, but the one left holding the unforgiveness is the one holding the pain. Forgiveness is the only way to be free from the past and the pain. Leaving the judgment in God's hands is a good place for it, since He is the only one truly righteous and fair. A wife's moving on brings peace to her like nothing else can. Even though she has scar tissue, it eventually will no longer hurt to the touch.

It's also important to understand that forgiveness does not mean remaining with an abusive person, or forgoing the pursuit of restitution if warranted, or having your say in court. It does mean that letting the natural consequences happen is for the other person's growth, not to make you feel better, fuel your revenge, or meet your need for justice.

Chances are, without our act of forgiving, we'd feel unsatisfied no matter what the legal outcomes. Families of murder victims sometimes wait months or years for justice. Yet even when the killer's punishment fits the crime, they often feel let down. Even if the criminal gets the death penalty, it won't bring their loved one back. The only way we can move on is through the emotional freedom of forgiving. Otherwise we feel like we're dragging around another person everywhere we go. Not only is it exhausting, the burden impacts everything else we do and all our other relationships.

It takes time to grow wings. The larva of the firefly grows it wings inside its cocoon. The space between your anger and your willingness to let God's grace work in you might be compared to a cocoon, and spinning that cocoon is hard work. So you need to do the work, and then be patient. Like the larva prior to its transformation, you cannot know how free those wings will make you feel until you try them out. You might have to take my word for it at first, but once you take flight and experience the wind beneath your wings, you'll understand that forgiving has given you freedom. The first step is being willing; let God do the rest.

Here are some more glimmers as you spin that cocoon.

- Forgiveness is a choice, not a feeling.
- Forgiveness is a process.
- We are called by God to forgive.
- Unforgiveness stalls growth and turns us bitter.
- Fly on the wings of freedom.

Path Lights

Don't pick on people, jump on their failures, criticize their faults—unless, of course, you want the same treatment. Don't condemn those who are down; that hardness can boomerang. (Luke 6:37)

Let me give you a new command: Love one another. In the same way I loved you, you love one another. This is how everyone will recognize that you are my disciples—when they see the love you have for each other. (John 13:34–35)

Basically, all of us, whether insiders or outsiders, start out in identical conditions, which is to say that we all start out as sinners. Scripture leaves no doubt about it. (Rom. 3:9)

> Fortunate those whose crimes are carted off,
>   whose sins are wiped clean from the slate.
> Fortunate the person against
>   whom the Lord does not keep score.
>   (Rom. 4:7–8)

Make a clean break with all cutting, backbiting, profane talk. Be gentle with one another, sensitive. Forgive one another as quickly and thoroughly as God in Christ forgave you. (Eph. 4:31–32)

Be even-tempered, content with second place, quick to forgive an offense. Forgive as quickly and completely as the Master forgave you. And regardless of what else you put on, wear love. It's your basic, all-purpose garment. Never be without it. (Col. 3:13–14)

Journaling

It's time to get away and spend some time reflecting on your books. These are not physical books, but your emotional bookkeeping system. Ask God to show you if you're holding anything against someone else. The goal is to be in balance—nothing owed and nothing owing. So much as it's in your power to be at peace with others, just do it. The first step may simply be to agree with God that a deficit exists, then let Him show you how to let it go. Or He may ask you to go to another person and ask for his or her forgiveness. Remember, God will give you the strength and provide the way.

CHAPTER 9

Prisms

Accepting God's Design

Once the rays of God's love are allowed to penetrate the heart, the old gloomy pits are flooded with light. We climb out of darkness, lit up by God's grace, and start to spread a little of that light ourselves. Like sunlight through a *prism*, Christ's love, when held up to the raindrops in our hearts, is refracted into new colors—sparkles of love, joy, peace, patience, kindness, goodness, faithfulness, gentleness, and self-control.

The significance of God's rainbow in the book of Genesis is His promise. His promises become personal to me as I feel His intimate care in the hard times. Now, when I see a colorful arc paint our Northwest sky, I thank God for His love, grace, and hope.

Each rainbow is slightly different. They vary in size, the width of each band of color, and even the number of identifiable hues. But the right combination of rain and sun bends the light and reveals the different tones. When, for instance, my life is positioned in the midst of God's light, I see His rays of hope. The irony is that it's painful. It takes what you might call a precipitation of our spiritual tears, refracting the light of God's love into a reflection of all His glory. So all of us have the potential to reflect the myriad of God's character traits. We are all uniquely beautiful.

Before I go any further, it's important that I define a word that is grossly misunderstood. *Beauty*, by the world's standard, has come to mean something narrow, superficial, and completely opposite of God's original plan. In each of us, God has created a magnificent and complete masterpiece, and He has carefully applied each artful brushstroke. Even more amazing, God incorporates those marks we bear that have been made by the Enemy—marks intended to mar His design.

As with any masterpiece, our beauty and worth have nothing to do with the paint, oil, or canvas, but everything to do with the Master who created us. God's beauty never fades, and that loveliness is the unique light that shines from every human soul. This light represents the eternal part of us that longs to be recognized and used according to the Creator's master plan. No one else possesses the exquisiteness that is yours.

This may be the first time you've heard this truth. You may have a hard time seeing your own beauty at first. Like an impressionist painting, up close the brushstrokes seem random and indistinct. Step back, and the image becomes clearer. At one time, I could have rattled off a whole list of reasons why the words *beauty* or *exquisiteness* did not apply to me. I never knew this truth—that no perceived weakness or flaw could reduce my beauty. The Creator of the world wonderfully made you and me, knowing every detail of our lives. No mistake. Take a moment and really meditate on this truth. Don't wait to feel that it's true—decide it is today.

Please don't skip over this important step. A few women have admitted to me that it was easy to believe God loved others, but not them. This is a lie from the very pit of hell. Believing this lie keeps you at arms length from your heavenly Father. This Father is the only one who loves you perfectly, completely, and without conditions. He may or may not have been reflected in your earthly father—a man, after all, who could give only what he possessed himself. It may be time to take the hopes and dreams in relation to your earthly father and place them in the one Father who has everything you need. He longs to bless you.

We live in a tragic world, have you noticed? There is One who is bigger than the biggest obstacle, trial, or injury. God is the only one who can bring beauty from ashes. Give Him your ashes.

From the moment of our birth, the world's negative messages about beauty chip away at God's truth. It will take some time to repair the damage. When we believe our self-worth depends on external traits, our image of self is in a downward spiral. It starts, perhaps, when the pretty "blue-eyed girl" gets more attention, or the "slow" child receives negative attention. Then some other child, out of his or her own pain, points out physical differences we may have. Add to that the careless words of family members, and the spiral continues downward. The hiding, changing, shrinking, and hurting leads us further into darkness.

At this point, we need divine intervention. Without it, energy that should be put into getting to know our Savior is spent on clothes, makeup, surgery, diets, exercise, and every self-improvement book we can read. Oh how this must break the heart of the One who created us to be the way we are for His divine purpose.

This tendency to be critical of our bodies is often fanned into a raging fire when our husbands betray us. The lie screams in our minds that we are to blame. I understand, having spent some time in the heat of this battle. Many husbands, too, apply their own brand of blame in an attempt to avoid taking responsibility.

I was working on self-image issues, studying the Bible, and reading lots of books. I knew the truth even though I didn't feel it when I looked in the mirror. Then my husband's addiction came out, and I went right back to the lie. It took a lot of work and being reminded by God, over and over, to recognize how wrong I was.

Now, after I've walked with so many women through a husband's betrayal, I clearly see that the facts don't support the lie. The women who have been through my support group are beautiful, vibrant, and talented. They come in every shape and size, believing their husbands' addictions were their fault. I realized then that my husband's baggage belongs to him, and mine belongs to me. And though we each have our own baggage, they are often coordinating. It isn't up to him to make me feel attractive. I must know who I am in Christ.

Tammy continued to walk with her friend. The friend's husband was not willing to make any changes, and his resistance was taking its toll on her.

My friend was talking about how her husband's sexual addiction had really done a number on her self-esteem. I felt prompted to speak the truth, but I was worried how she'd take it. The question seemed to jump out of my mouth, and then it sat there between us for what felt like forever.

"How do you think your attractiveness ties into your husband's addiction?"

Her face showed her annoyance and she said, "Well, of course, when your husband strays you can't help but wonder, 'What was wrong with me?'"

I felt like a hypocrite, so I said, "Oh, yes—I felt the same way, and I still fight the doubts, even though I know the truth."

"What truth?"

"Sexual addiction starts when men are young boys, before they ever meet their wives. This addiction is not about sex or attractiveness. Look at the news. Look at the beautiful models and stars whose husbands have cheated on them. The more I read, the more I see that all addictions are all about medicating pain and escaping."

"Pain? What pain?"

"Deep, emotional hurts . . . like abuse, abandonment, critical or absent parents, any number of injuries that are too deep for a child to process." There was a long pause. Another question seemed to slip out of my mouth. "Why do you think your husband turned to porn?" I could see the wheels turning, and then a large tear fell from her eye, missed her cheek altogether, and fell onto her lap.

She whispered her reply, "Because when my husband looks at other women, he thinks they're everything I'm not."

It was a powerful moment for both of us. I understood the sting of feeling insecure whenever an attractive woman walked by. I tried to live up to some ridiculous standard myself and then just gave it up as hopeless. Thankfully, the lie lost a bit more power as we took it out and looked at it under the light of truth. God reminded me of His Word that says I am wonderfully made. I shared that truth with my friend, and we were both encouraged.

I even took a chance and shared our conversation with my husband when he called that night. Defensiveness or blame had been his usual pattern, but I recognized a softness and empathy as he realized another piece of the pain he'd caused. This was new.

<hr>

Stephanie had always been confident and "together"—on the outside. She worked hard at the illusion, convincing herself that she was in control. This new place of being, led by God's Spirit, still left her feeling uneasy.

I got up this morning with all my plans put into place. As I packed my bags, the tears flowed freely with all the old hopes and dreams I'd wrapped up in my husband. When I finally told him my plan, he simply said, "Do what you feel you must."

Making those preparations to leave my husband and my home caused fear to well up within me. How would I manage financially? How would I feel without male companionship in my life? I wasn't young. Who would want another person's castoffs? Tears moved to sobs as I reached for my Bible. I opened it, and my eyes fell on Isaiah 54:4–5. God said that I would not suffer shame, and He was my husband. So I continued to pack but purposely leaving out fear.

One week after moving into my new place, I was feeling stronger. God was meeting all my needs: financial, practical, emotional, and spiritual. Every time I looked at His Book, went to church, or listened to our local Christian radio station, He spoke directly to me.

Then the papers arrived from my husband's lawyer. He'd filed for divorce first. The old fears came back. The words "God hates divorce" shouted in my head. I immediately called my group leader. I didn't want to go backward.

That woman was Jesus to me when I needed Him. She prayed with me, reminding me of His amazing love for my husband and me. Then she said the most powerful words: "God doesn't desire divorce any more than He wants us to have pain. He loves His children; He loves divorced people." Now when the old lie comes back to mind, I answer with, "God loves divorced people, and God loves me."

Renee had turned a corner, allowing God to change her heart and soften her temperament. She was ready to face this new challenge and take the next step of faith.

When I called my husband to set up a time to meet, I could sense he felt uncertain. He asked if he should bring his lawyer. I said, "Three's a crowd," and then I suggested, in my sultriest voice, that we meet at our old favorite restaurant where we used to go for romantic dinners. His voice softened as he said, "I'd love to."

I looked forward to it, but I still had to push back those old fears of rejection. I again picked out one of his favorite outfits to wear and took my time getting ready. I felt like a teenager getting ready for her first date. Even my sons let out a whistle when I came downstairs. I could feel that they were hopeful, too, about tonight, though we hadn't discussed it. I didn't know what to say to them. I didn't want to give them any false hope—or to have any myself.

When I walked into the restaurant, I could actually feel

my heart beating in my chest. I can't remember the last time that happened. When I saw my husband stand, and I saw the look of love on his face, the icy-hard edges that had built up between us melted. I still loved this man. After I'd gone through so much turmoil, this was a welcome calm.

The conversation between us was easy and not tense. We talked about what we'd been doing in our separate lives, about the boys, and about God. This was a new man. He was taking responsibility for his life and for his choices—and he was choosing to grow stronger.

We both agreed it was time for him to come back home. We'll just take it one day at a time and put Christ at the center for the first time ever. I'm full of hope and thankfulness.

❧

This concept of beauty continues to be distorted. The number of women, particularly young women, who have plastic surgery is growing each year. While I don't necessarily condemn plastic surgery or the women who choose it, my heart breaks over this growing trend that seems to reinforce the lie that our value as women is based on our attractiveness—or lack of it. Too much emphasis is placed on this external shell and not enough on the eternal soul contained within.

Trying to fix the void in our hearts, from the outside, is nothing new. Chemicals, drugs, food, status, shopping, image, beauty, gambling, sex, busyness—all are as empty as the internal void feels. Nothing on the list will satisfy for any length of time. Only God can give us eternal satisfaction, because He designed us to need Him alone—to be the only one who can fill our emptiness. And we need filling—the filling of God's pure love. It's the only remedy that brings permanent satisfaction.

So why aren't all believers blissfully satisfied the instant they accept Christ? Because we bring our baggage with us. I came to God, desiring His peace and perfection. I assumed that, as a believer, I was changed. And I was—to God. My heavenly Father saw me through the shed blood of Christ. I was accepted and cleared of all charges, but still broken and burdened with baggage. I spent a lot of time trying to fit God into my baggage. He was, and is, patient with me because the process of becoming spiritually mature takes time. Each day I need to make a choice—serve God and learn to adjust to my new life in Him. I have to allow Christ to live through me. Some days I make the unfortunate choice to stay right where I am.

When couples enter marriage, we have much to learn about each other. We each need to make adjustments in order for the relationship to grow and survive. Prior to the wedding, we have only our thoughts or assumptions about wedded life—"I will always love my spouse, and my spouse will always love me." But from experience, we learn the truth about marriage—"Why did you disagree with me in front of my mother? You're always supposed to take my side!" Many of our initial ideas are confirmed, of course—"I like having someone to eat dinner with every evening." But new information is added too: "I didn't know that about you" is a common phrase. Some discoveries are easier to absorb than others—"Your favorite color is blue?" But all change the relationship—"You're right. I won't do that again."

As a new believer, the more I learned about God, Jesus, and the Holy Spirit, the more I wanted to know. As wonderful as it was to read about God's love and provision, it was even more amazing to experience it. These experiences revealed both the correct and incorrect assumptions I had about God. They changed our relationship and they revealed baggage that needed to go. The more I saw God, the clearer my own reflection was.

This painful process of reflection showed me how much energy I spent on the people around me: "I wonder what they must think of me" or "I hope my spouse's new boss doesn't think that I'm not sophisticated." These doubts came from the wrong assumption that my self-worth would come from others; my value would either be bestowed upon me or diminished by the people around me. Having to be what others expect is impossible. Often I ended up looking foolish and putting my heart under the feet of everyone else. I even worried about what a casual bystander might think.

A close cousin of worrying about what others thought was the propensity to compare myself to others. Both activities kept my eyes to the left or right of me instead of looking up at Christ. Now I know that when I compare it brings despairs so I don't go there.

Before God revealed otherwise to me, I assumed thoughtfulness and caring were my motivation for expending so much energy. I thought my intuition allowed me to be a considerate and compassionate friend. I was also a doormat. My being easily swayed or manipulated made it easy for some cruel people to impose on me, and created self-made pain. When there were strains in a relationship, I assumed it was my fault. Somehow I was responsible for others' feelings. My poor children were simply an extension of me. If they misbehaved, it meant I was a bad mother. Choosing to carry the world on my shoulders was exhausting and futile. It's impossible to be all things to all people.

I still wrestle with wanting to impress others. God does a good job pointing this out. Say, for example, I'm looking for kudos in a particular setting—"The ladies altar committee will be so impressed with this flower arrangement." Instead, I may get criticism: "What? You say purple lilacs clash with the altar cloth?" I sulk a bit, and then realize again that the only one I need to please is Christ—"I want the altar arrangement to reflect the love Jesus and I have for one another." He loves me too much to feed any desire other than my desire for Him.

When I go into a situation as a confident ambassador of Christ, looking to be a reflection of what He is and looking for nothing more, that's when the kudos come. The irony is, I don't need the kudos, so I thank God and pass it back to the One who deserves the praise. What makes the difference? In the first scenario, I try to prove my worth. In the second, I know my worth and from where it comes—Christ.

There's a fine line between having low self-worth and being self-focused or narcissistic. The line is humility. On the one side I'm striving to prove my worth by battling the lies that say I'm worthless. The other side says I decide my worth through fame, fortune, image, intellect, and so forth. In the middle is truth. My worth is priceless based solely on my Creator. This truth is a great equalizer because it's true for all. My worth is not more or less than anyone else's. We are nothing except what we allow Christ to be in us. My understanding that I have nothing to offer apart from Jesus *and* unlimited potential in Him brings peace, freedom, purpose, and worth. Here are some glimmers to light up your self-worth.

- I am God's creation.
- All of God's children are precious.
- My beauty is eternal.
- My value is secure.
- Apart from Christ I can do nothing.

Path Lights

GOD formed Man out of dirt from the ground and blew into his nostrils the breath of life. The Man came alive—a living soul! (Gen. 2:7)

Your vibrant beauty has gotten inside us—
    you've been so good to us! We're walking on air!
All we are and have we owe to GOD,
    Holy God of Israel, our King!
                     (Ps. 89:17–18)

So thank GOD for his marvelous love,
    for his miracle mercy to the children he loves.
He poured great draughts of water down parched throats;
    the starved and hungry got plenty to eat.
                     (Ps. 107:8–9)

But don't, dear friend, resent GOD's discipline;
    don't sulk under his loving correction.
It's the child he loves that GOD corrects;
    a father's delight is behind all this.
                     (Prov. 3:11–12)

Good morning!
You're beautiful with God's beauty,
Beautiful inside and out!
God be with you.

(Luke 1:28)

I am the vine; you are the branches. If a man remains in me and I in him, he will bear much fruit; apart from me you can do nothing. (John 15:5 NIV)

Journaling

Write a list of all your best qualities. No negatives allowed. Ask God to guide this process and show you how He sees you. As you read about God's love for His children, His promises and plans, make it personal. Everything He has is for you! You are a masterpiece. Each time you look in a mirror say out loud, "I am fearfully and wonder-fully made"—own it!

Also beware of things that may trigger negative messages in your mind. At one time, whenever a clothing catalog came to my home, I sat down and poured over it, and my self-esteem plummeted. I never bought anything. Instead, each picture set a silent standard, evidence that I didn't live up. The result was always dissatisfaction with my figure, hair, clothes, makeup. I now immediately toss those catalogs without even looking at them. You, too, may need to put up boundaries if a critical thing or person in your life feeds the negative beast. Simply recognize that comments made by a person are more about his or her own issues and pain than about you. Learn to refuse to take them on. Then watch out for the comparison trap.

CHAPTER 10

Path Lights

The Road Ahead

At my first support group meeting, the leader put up a chart depicting the average time for healing. Looking at it then, the five-year estimate seemed like a lifetime. The thought of remaining in this place of pain for any length of time was unbearable. We can be thankful that this place of pain isn't constant for those five years. As with any healing process, the pain diminishes over time, and some level of normal function returns. There is, on the other hand, hard work and setbacks along the way. Now, past the five-year mark, I can say emphatically that the work is well worth doing and the payoff immeasurable.

It's good to have some idea what to expect. Of course, every situation has unique aspects. But, in general, the first year is the most difficult, made worse in the likely event of multiple relapses by the husband. Now, though, you have the tools from the previous chapters to help you cope. Some chapters are for now and others will make more sense when you're farther down the path to healing. There's a lot of information to absorb in these chapters, so come back to this book from time to time; different chapters will stand out.

Your journey on the path to healing is propelled forward when you come to understand that you can't control your spouse, and that your situation is not all about him. Your attitude sets the tone. Are you open? Or shut down and angry? Can your husband come to you without condemnation and wrath? Do you think that being open and receptive means what he did was okay? Having strong emotions is normal when we're in great pain, but there's a cost involved in not dealing well with our anger. Be aware of how toxic unresolved anger can be, a subject talked about in chapter 6. And dealing with anger is not a onetime deal. New layers of pain will be revealed, and then anger will again need to be dealt with.

Another key to the journey is to beware of out-of-balance times. They still come, though not as often and not always because of sexual addiction. These are times when you feel a growing dissatisfaction. I'm getting so that I can recognize them sooner rather than later. I become irritable, negative, judgmental, and unhappy. If I let those feelings go on too long, I'm paralyzed, not having the desire to do anything productive.

Becoming out of balance starts with one lie that sticks. For me, it's often about the importance of my appearance. If I don't track down that lie and treat it with the balm of God's truth, it festers. Soon the lie spreads, and there's another related lie, and then another, until I'm convinced that no one cares, not even God. My worthlessness is evident. Even as I type this, it's clear that these messages are really lies, which is a ridiculous state to be in, because I *know* the truth. When I'm into this negative condition, I can't see the truth. I try to pray but it feels futile. My mouth says, "It's not true," but my heart doesn't believe it.

So how do I get out? I have to acknowledge that I need help and then ask God to step in. Part of me doesn't want His help because I'm sure He will simply confirm what I already know—it's my fault, whatever it is. I'm forgetting in the moment that being convicted is not the same thing as being condemned. The voice condemning me for this pity party is not that of the Lord. God has to take me back to the place where the original lie first showed up. When I humble myself and ask, praying even when I don't feel like it, His Holy Spirit will show me.

I always have to go back to the basics: God loves me; He made me with a plan in mind; I can't work on the plan without Him. Then I count the many blessings, and look at all the times God was faithful in the past. Sometimes breakthrough comes quickly, sometimes it takes longer, but God always honors my request to get back onto His lap. The one thing I have noticed is breakthroughs are usually predicated by breakdowns.

Truth is the medicine that treats lies. Stay in the arena of truth. Some truth, however, is harder to accept at first. I remember when it dawned on me that, even though my husband was getting help and working on his issues, he could still fall. I saw the men who tried and failed—over and over. These men are forever one poor choice away from slipping right back into their addiction. This truth created a wall of fear that closed in on me whenever my husband traveled. Then God gently showed me that the potential for betrayal is a reality in every relationship and every person. Even if I divorced my husband and remarried, I'd get another person with baggage. My faith had to be placed in God and no one else.

Once I shifted all of my hope and placed it in God, I saw Him at work in my husband. The light came on. As long as I put my faith in Christ, whose work is being reflected in my husband, we would all be in balance—Christ, my husband, and me. When a doubt tries to creep in, I recall the recent ways that Christ has been evident in my husband. Then I visualize Jesus right there with him wherever he is. Finally, I thank Him for being faithful to let me know anything I need to know.

As I reflect back over the last five years, I'm in awe of all that God has accomplished in my relationship with Him. Not that I've arrived, but I'm moving forward. God has used my fears and shame to show me new depths of His amazing love and character. Each new revelation of Him encourages me to continue to get to know Him. Only God could take a woman with her head down in shame and make her a mouthpiece for the very subject that caused her shame in the first place.

The experience of betrayal and discovery has also shown me something for my two daughters. They were in their teens when their lives took this unexpected turn. I'll never forget the day their dad shattered their idealistic world for good. Like me, they had put him on a pedestal—one needing to be knocked over so that God could take center stage in their lives. Now, when they go into relationships with men, they are more well grounded in reality and equipped with knowledge. I'm truly thankful that they are also stronger having gone through the pain.

I regret the years I sent them mixed messages. I spent so much time telling the girls about God and talking about right from wrong—all the while modeling codependency. The added benefit of letting God change me is the ripple effects on those around me. What a waste of energy it is, trying to change someone. But change yourself, and you give others permission and a map to do the same.

This truth came home a couple of years ago when I was working on my computer. My youngest daughter was home watching Oprah. My oldest, while away at college, called to see if I was watching Oprah. Now this was not uncommon since we used to watch the show together when she was home. Many good mother-daughter conversations came out of the show's topics. I told her that Sarah was watching, but I was working.

She explained that there was a young woman on the show who was a beautiful model. This young woman shared her sad secret with viewers—that she had always had low self-esteem and couldn't believe it when others told her how gorgeous she was. She prayed to God, asking that, for just ten minutes, she could see herself the way others saw her. My daughter, who was crying, said she felt the same way. I often wondered why my daughters, both beautiful inside and out, didn't seem to know it. I told them all the time that they were beautiful. So I turned off the computer and went into the other room. There, my youngest sat on the couch with tears running down her face.

As I watched that show, God turned the light on me. That lovely model could not see herself as beautiful because her own mother didn't see herself that way. She'd passed it on, and so had I. It grieved my heart when I realized my years of struggling with body image issues had been passed on, even though I tried hard not to saddle my daughters with such a negative legacy. I turned to Sarah—with

Laurel on the phone—and apologized for not treating myself with more respect. I said, "All three of us are beautiful women." Then I made a promise to myself and to them: I will do my best to grow old gracefully so that they can, too.

Betrayed women who have children often debate over how much to tell them about the state of the household—and when. Every situation is unique, and I say again, let God lead the way. This means fear and shame no longer get a voice. Honesty is never a mistake. I guarantee your kids know something is wrong no matter what their ages. You might say simply, "Mommy and Daddy are having trouble in their marriage, but we're committed to working it out. Pray for us." Then let their questions dictate any more to be said. The older the child, the more questions he or she will have. If you aren't sure about the answers, tell that child, "I'm not sure." You don't have to have all the answers. Trust God to guide the timing and the telling. Then point your children ever back to their only perfect parent—Jesus Christ.

Every woman who comes to the support group wants to be sure whatever she shares will be kept confidential. The shame runs deep. Most of us have spent a lot of time making sure everything looks good from the outside. It took years to tell some of our family members. I still worry about what people will think. So why write a book? Simple—because God has turned the shame into something very positive, and I want the world to know. He has given me the ability to put words on a page, and He has guided the process.

You, however, or any other woman you know, have the right to withhold or to share information with family and friends, or even the world, as you see fit. Any sharing must be led by God. Some women come to the support group for help and then move on in a healthy way, having told few others. Whether or not you share, be careful that the decision is between you and God only. I'm pretty sure that in the beginning I would not have signed up to be the poster child for betrayal through sexual addiction. But God showed me, one hurting woman at I time, how sharing my experience could encourage other women. As you get stronger, don't be surprised what God will do through you.

Tammy's, Stephanie's, and Renee's stories have left off in what may feel like the middle. Well, that's the way it is in real life—little can be wrapped up with a bow or the statement, "They lived happily ever after." Not even Renee has that guarantee. What I hope you did see were three different situations, ways to respond, and results; this is reality. Not every husband gets help or gets better, but every woman who reaches out for Christ will find Him, and in Christ is all hope.

This is not a sentiment that breaks down under pressure—it is truth. Every time I see a court decision that protects a woman and her children; every time a husband who, in his addiction, lets his wife have more than the court would; whenever God shows His miraculous provision when nothing seems to be in a wife's favor—I am humbled again at His amazing grace. I've seen too much to doubt God's ability on your behalf.

It's hard for me to say when His love was most beautiful—when Christ took the dark places in my life and used them to deepen my understanding, or when He painted a golden stroke of blessing in a lavish act of love on the cross. Both changed me. It's all evidence of my need for Him in plenty and in want. I can't wait for the next brushstroke.

Remember that healing is a process. At the end of this book you'll still have pain and your own dark pits. But be encouraged—God loves you too much to leave you there. Everything and more that He has done for me and the women I know will be done for you. It goes back to what I said in the introduction: the more energy you put into the process of knowing God and through Him knowing healing, the more you will benefit. There will be dark pits, but much light also.

Time and truth will shed new light on your situation. God will take what was intended for evil and use it for good. Your story will no longer be one of shame and fear, but of victory over pain. I trust that God will provide everything you need for the journey ahead, and pray that this book was a beacon of hope along the way. Here are some ideas and our final glimmers. Don't worry, there are plenty more where they came from!

- Take the practical next step.
- Give yourself grace.

- Condemnation is not from God.
- No situation is too big for Christ.

Here are a few ideas for the next step.

1. Stay in God's presence with continued alone time, journaling, and reading His Word.
2. If you are not part of a church family, look for the right one.
3. Look for support groups in your area like S-Anon, or log on to online support at www.settingcaptivesfree.com—Online Courses: Sexual Purity: "A United Front."
4. Find a biblical Christian counselor. Before you call, pray! Also it is a good idea to formulate a list of questions to ask each counselor. It's important to let God guide you to the right person.

Sample questions:

- Will you pray with me?
- Will you see my husband later?
- Do you take my insurance?
- Have you dealt much with _____ (fill in the blank with the issue you face)?

Path Lights

Listen carefully to my wisdom; take to heart what I can teach you. You'll treasure its sweetness deep within; you'll give it bold expression in your speech. To make sure your foundation is trust in God, I'm laying it all out right now just for you. (Prov. 22:17–19)

It's urgent that you listen carefully to this: Anyone here who believes what I am saying right now and aligns himself with the Father, who has in fact put me in charge, has at this very moment the real, lasting life and is no longer condemned to be an outsider. This person has taken a giant step from the world of the dead to the world of the living. (John 5:24)

Don't burn out; keep yourselves fueled and aflame. Be alert servants of the Master, cheerfully expectant. Don't quit in hard times; pray all the harder. (Rom. 12:11–12)

Be a lifelong learner—stay in process.

Journaling

Take some time for yourself and dream. Write out a prayer to God regarding what your ideal future looks like. Be honest about the things that feel too big as well as the promises in God's Word that are hard to believe right now. Step out in faith and tell God what you need—be specific.

Next, take a look inward at your gifts, abilities, and unspoken loves. Imagine a future with unlimited potential and resources; then imagine yourself there. What would you be doing? Would you write, paint, teach, learn to fly, ski, or dance?

Whatever your dream activity or job is, whisper it to God and write it down as a request between you and Him. Now listen for His voice and wait for the answer with an expectant heart. He is a Father who loves to give good gifts to His children—that's you!

CHAPTER 11

Refraction

My Husband's Perspective

You may still have a few questions. Maybe I can answer some of them. I have a lot of practice answering questions. You see, two to three times a year, I, along with two other leaders from our For Men Only (FMO) group (see appendix B), show up for each new session of the Healing Hearts class. Our purpose is to answer the ladies' questions regarding their husband's sexual addiction. FMO meets at our church and is a place for men to find healing, answers, and accountability in dealing with their sexual addiction. When Meg asked me to write the last chapter of this book, I thought the best thing I could do was provide you with answers to some of the most common questions posed by women who are in the same situation. First let me give you some background.

I'll never forget the first time I went to a Healing Hearts session. I was anxious because I expected the women to be angry. Not at me but at men in general. I anticipated that I'd be walking into a hostile environment. Yes, there were a couple of ladies who were angry. I could see it on their faces. But what I saw more clearly was their pain. In addition to the pain, fear, and anger, there was something else—love. This was unexpected.

No one verbally expressed it, but it was there. It showed up in their tears and was present in their questions. Love was evident in their desire to know why their husbands were behaving this way. And there was something else. I could feel it. These women wanted answers, but what they wanted most was hope—hope that their marriages could be restored and that love could survive, hope that their husbands could find healing, and hope that somehow the world would make sense again.

If I may, let me stand in the gap and say I'm truly sorry your husband has betrayed you. You did nothing to cause this nor was there anything you could have done to prevent it. Although you've been deeply affected by your husband's poor choices and behavior, they are his alone. I need to reiterate that your husband's sexual addiction (SA) has nothing to do with sex. It has everything to do with avoidance of pain (medicating) and addiction. Your husband, at a very early age, discovered that sex, more specifically the chemicals released in his body during sexual activity, are a way of coping with the "issues" in his life. One of the lies sexual addicts believe is "sex is my single greatest need." One reason SA is different than other addictions (alcohol, drugs, food, work, etc.) is the greater havoc and destruction caused on a relational level. Scripture tells us that "all other sins a man commits are outside his body, but he who sins sexually sins against his own body" (1 Cor. 6:18 NIV). It's important that you know that you are not to blame.

Here are some questions I've received from women in the same circumstance. I hope my answers will help you understand a bit more about what you and your husband are dealing with.

How do you feel about Meg writing this book?

At first I was hesitant and fearful. The prospect of having thousands of people knowing my story was overwhelming. I prayed and sought God's direction. I discussed it with a few very close friends and ultimately decided I had to trust God and surrender to His will. I have to confess that my main concern was selfish: "What about my reputation?" Once I turned that over to God, the decision was easy. Let God do His work . . . taking what was meant for evil and using it for good.

It amazes me that, the first time I shared a bit of my story, a number of men said that they've struggled with pornography. I'm not alone nor is my situation unique—sexual addiction is more prevalent than you might think. The only way to start dealing with it is by having it exposed and discussed. I can't change what has happened, and I'll always regret the choices I've made. But I can also continue to move forward, focus on, and share the amazing grace that God bestows upon us all.

Can you pinpoint when it all began?

Every man I've talked with knows when his SA started. For most it began when they were around ten years of age, and they found their father's stash of pornography. For some the beginning was after one or both parents abused them sexually, physically, or mentally. The most common starting point has been after viewing porn. The fastest growing trend has young men telling me that their problem started after viewing porn on the computer. The introduction of the Internet has made hard-core porn accessible to anyone twenty-four hours a day in the privacy of his or her own room.

When I was about ten, I found a stash of pornography (*Playboy*, *Hustler*, and X-rated novels). Up until that point I'd never seen pictures of a nude woman. I can still remember the rush of adrenaline and other chemicals surging through my brain and body. I'd instantly found the answer to my loneliness. Or at least I thought so. What I didn't expect was the intense sense of guilt and shame that followed.

Both of my parents were in their forties when I was born, and by this time I was on my own quite often. My middle sister was still living at home but working and going to college. As I discovered during counseling for my SA, one of my "triggers" was feeling lonely. Triggers are the things that set off the SA cycle. Triggers vary, but most include being hungry, angry, lonely, and tired. Strong emotions can be a trigger. Men typically don't connect the triggers to their addiction. That's why counseling and/or involvement in a support group is essential. Once I was able to identify loneliness as a trigger,

I could fight the feeling with the fact that I'm never really alone. God is always with me. I've learned to appreciate this fact, and it has given me great comfort.

A common thinking error that men fall prey to is, *Someone else is at fault.* Blaming my dad for years was easy. He wasn't there. The lie was, if he'd been more in tune and available for those critical conversations, I never would have gotten "hooked." The truth is, if it hadn't started then, it would have started later. Only recently have I discovered how my choices caused or worsened life's difficulties. I picked the escape route. Many of my friends while growing up turned to alcohol or drugs. Every step of the way I made choices to continue with my addiction and knew these choices were wrong. The guilt kept me in hiding and going back.

Why didn't my husband tell me about his problem before?

Most likely he believed that you'd walk out on him. I remember being nudged by the Holy Spirit to tell Meg about my addiction before it had progressed, early on in our marriage. I truly believed she'd run out of the room screaming, and our marriage would end. One of the differences between SA and other forms of addiction is the shame and guilt that are associated with it. Today, when people admit to being an alcoholic or a drug addict, they're celebrated for their courage in admitting their struggles. That's just not the case for men struggling with SA. Not only do men have a sense of guilt and shame about their addiction, society denies it's even an addiction. People either laugh and make jokes or automatically assume all men with SA are child molesters or predators.

Most men get caught. Some confess before their secret life is exposed. For me, the turning point came after another "failure." I distinctly remember confessing to God that I couldn't go on any longer. At that moment I felt God turn away, and I felt a deep sense of loneliness—loneliness so complete it scared me. Then I felt God's presence again. At that moment He showed me that I'd never truly been alone. He had always been there. He also told me it was time to tell Meg everything. I knew the only way I could get on the path to recovery was by meeting my shame and guilt head-on. It was time for these dark feelings to see the light of day. The hardest thing I've ever done in my entire life was to tell Meg everything!

Do I need to know everything?

The answer is yes and no. Your husband does need to tell you everything, especially if he's had physical contact with another person. As hard as it will be to hear, it's important for two reasons. One, it's for your safety so you'll know what you have been exposed to. And two, it's the only way your husband will be able to start the recovery process.

When God finally broke through to me, two things entered my mind. Meg's health was potentially at risk, and God was still in control. He assured me the right thing to do was to tell Meg everything—even though there was a chance that being totally honest could mean the end of our marriage. I then had an overwhelming sense of peace. Regardless of whether or not Meg and I would remain husband and wife, I knew in my heart and soul that we'd be okay. For the first time in my life, I knew I could tell someone my complete story.

While you want your husband to be totally honest with you and not to hold anything back, you don't need to know all of the details. One of the things that Meg regrets is asking about some of the particulars. One of the things I regret is not asking her sooner if she really wanted to know the facts of a particular situation. I was prepared to tell her anything she wanted to know. The problem was, by telling her some of the minutiae, it created an image in Meg's mind that she then had to deal with. While you don't need to know the specifics, you do need your husband to confess the avenue his addiction has gone (porn, prostitution, illegal activities, etc.) and a timeline. Any unconfessed area is a foothold for Satan to exploit. I can pinpoint times in my SA where it progressed, and these were directly related to times when I was not totally honest with Meg.

What goes through your mind as you continue in your addiction?

The most prevalent feeling is shame and guilt. Another lie that sexual addicts believe is, "If anyone really knew me, they wouldn't like me or want to be around me." Believing this lie is the foundation for the shame every sexual addict carries. Knowing that I truly wanted to stop doing what I was doing, and asking God countless times to help me to stop, yet continuing to "act out," was extremely frustrating and depressing. But the feelings were unbearable, knowing that what I was doing was wrong yet fearful for saying anything because I was sure people would be repulsed. Who would understand? I truly believed that if I told anyone, I'd be ostracized. The more alone and isolated I felt, the more I acted out.

Did you even think about your wife?

To be brutally honest, during the acting out phase of the addiction cycle, no. Addiction has to do with medicating pain. By the time an addict is in the acting out phase, he's long passed rational thought of any potential consequences. Where a man does think about his wife is during the shame and guilt cycle. He feels guilty about his behavior but feels powerless to stop. Shame is heaped on him by the Evil One, who tells him that breaking free is hopeless.

Through prayer and the resources available, including counseling, I learned how I could recognize what was going on before and during the addiction cycle. One of the things I learned was I had a choice. I wasn't powerless. I could choose my wife instead of the old ways of addiction. For the first time, I was able to see Meg as who she really is and God's blessing to me through her. He worked through her.

What was the turning point for you to come clean?

For me, the turning point came when God allowed me to reach a point where I knew if I didn't choose to seek help, I'd die. Not just emotional and spiritual death. I was on a path that would eventually lead to physical death. At the same time, God showed me that He would be there every step of the way. While He hadn't taken the addiction all away and healed me miraculously, He did assure me that He would help me through the healing process. By that time, by God's grace, I was already part of a For Men Only small group. The hard part was confessing my entire SA past to my accountability group and to Meg.

The turning point for most men is when they get caught either by their wives, their bosses, or by the police. You'd think this would be the moment when the truth would come out and the healing process would start. Unfortunately, this is not the case most of the time. Some men get defensive and are in complete denial. They try to shift the blame and are unwilling to admit the fact that they have a problem. Most try to minimize it by saying it's no big deal, and their behavior isn't hurting anyone.

Others come clean—but only partially. Remember, the shame and guilt portion of the SA cycle is so strong, a man believes if he tells everything to his wife or to a friend, the person will "run screaming into the night." The problem is compounded when the addict offers only a partial disclosure, because there's a good chance the SA will progress to even greater depravity. This may happen over a short or long period of time—weeks, months, or even years. Over the course of a couple of years, I was given the opportunity to tell Meg everything. But out of fear, I partially disclosed. I shared just enough of my SA past to resolve whatever was the current issue. I can pinpoint these two events on a timeline, and they correspond to when my SA progressed to new levels. Unfortunately, each time the level was even lower.

Regardless of how a guy gets to his turning point, the critical step to his healing is his being 100 percent truthful with his wife. Omitting anything at this point is like leaving a crowbar for Satan; he'll use it as leverage, and the shame and guilt cycle will continue. There are many good resources on the subject of sexual addiction for both the husband and wife to read. There are also Christian counselors available, which is a wise choice for the husband and/or wife, either as a couple or individually. Being part of a group like For Men Only can be a tremendous help. The churches in your area may not offer this type of group. There are resources on the Internet and there are support groups like SA anonymous (see appendix B).

What could I have done to prevent all this?

Nothing.

As Meg has mentioned in this book, your husband was already heading down this path long before you met him. Every guy that I've spoken with can identify a time around eight or ten years of age when his SA started. My addiction started because I found a way to medicate away my pain and loneliness. Over time, more baggage got piled on, of course, but loneliness was my main trigger. I see now that God was trying to draw me closer to Him. I wasn't a believer, but I knew deep down that what I was doing wasn't right. All I knew was it alleviated the pain temporarily like drugs, alcohol, or any other addiction.

I can't stress this enough: your husband's addiction does not have anything to do with you. It has nothing to do with how you look, how available you are to him sexually, your personality, your weight, height, or the color of your hair. One lie perpetuated even by some counselors and pastors is if you'd be more available sexually, your husband wouldn't have to go elsewhere. Let me say again, this is uncategorically a lie based on total ignorance of the pathophysiology of sexual addiction. Meg and I had, what I thought, was a good sex life all while I was "knee-deep" in my SA.

What can I do to support my husband's healing?

You can't make the choice for him to get better. Regardless of whether he's made that choice, your main job is to get healthy yourself and pray for your husband. Learning the truth will enable you to set boundaries to protect yourself. I'll never forget the time Meg heard from God to set a boundary regarding how she responded to my outbursts of anger. For many years I used anger as a way to control her. One evening, as I was reacting angrily, Meg's response changed.

Instead of backing down and placating me to avoid the situation, she was quiet. Later, she told me that she heard God tell her to not react but to remain silent. This had a huge impact on me because all of a sudden what used to work didn't.

I actually thought I was going out of my mind. What was happening? Why isn't this working anymore? God actually was able to give me a new perspective on how I was behaving. This was a significant turning point for me, because Meg was willing to listen to God and change her reaction. Another boundary she set was if I continued to react angrily, I'd have to leave. Again, God was using the boundaries Meg was setting to give me His perspective on how destructive my behavior was. These boundaries aren't only to protect you, they can help your husband.

Every human being has to deal with the fact that we live in a broken world. Everyone is dealing with some problem or issue. We're either in a crisis, coming out of a crisis, or moving toward a crisis. This isn't a glass-half-empty perspective—it's reality. How we choose to work through the brokenness is the key to our living a healthy and abundant life—the life God promises through His Son. My prayer is that, through this book, you're beginning to see how God wants to work in you and through you without regard to what your husband does or does not do.

Right now praying for your husband may be the farthest thing from your mind. Divorce or causing him bodily harm may be the thoughts that are in the forefront of your mind. I can understand that. I knew that there was a good chance my marriage was going to end based on the choices I made. If I ever choose to go back to my SA, my marriage will most likely end. The bottom line is, your pain is real. I know that it isn't easy for you to pray for your husband, because it's hard to pray for the people who hurt us. I can say, though, because of Meg's determination to pray for my healing and for me, I was able to continue on the path of recovery. There were times when she'd pray for me before we went to bed. There were many more times when I felt her prayers as I went through my day.

The power of a praying wife should not be underestimated. Your prayers are important. They will lift up your husband as he pushes through the lies of the Enemy, and they will give him strength to work on his recovery. Your prayers will also be a powerful tool to help your husband if he's in denial or unwilling to start the process of recovery. Please believe me that God will bring your husband to a point of decision. Your husband will decide either to continue on his path of self-destruction or he'll decide to get healthy. You can't make that decision for him. But you can pray that he'll be receptive to what God is trying to do in his life. Your prayers and the prayers of others will play an incredibly important role in God's getting your partner's attention.

How will I know if my husband is getting healthy?

The first marker of healthiness is honesty. For years, your husband has been living a lie. He's used lying as a way to keep you and others from knowing who he really is. One of the lies he probably believes is that if any one truly knew him, no one would want to be around him. So his lying is a defense mechanism, and he's perfected it over many years. As he moves along on the journey to healing, he'll learn that honesty is essential to his recovery.

Secondly, is he growing closer to God? You see, divine power is the key to your husband's recovery. Sure, there have been guys who have mastered their sexual addiction on their own. They've hung on for dear life, trying to manage their addiction. Changing behavior, however, is only part of the healing process. If the guy hasn't started to deal with his heart issues, then it's only a matter of time before a relapse occurs. Only God can show a person what is in his—or her—heart, and only God can give a person the strength and wisdom to deal with these heart issues.

Lastly, are you seeing real change? Is he more attentive to your needs? Is he trying to really see you? Is he trying to connect emotionally, spiritually, and not just physically? Is he becoming the spiritual leader that God has called him to be?

All of this takes time. Don't expect your husband to be miraculously healed. He's going to stumble and fail. The important thing is that he's serious about continuing on the road to recovery, and he's sharing with you what's going on during his journey.

Remember, you are not responsible for your husband's successes or failures during his recovery process. While he should be honestly sharing with you what's going on, you are not his accountability partner. It's not your job to monitor your husband's recovery. If he doesn't know another man whom he can be accountable to, pray that God will provide such an individual. Just as your husband is responsible for the choices he's made during his battle with sexual addiction, he alone is responsible for his recovery.

Leave your husband's addiction and his recovery in the hands of God. And you should not expect to find *your* hope in your husband's recovery. The most important thing for you is to take care of yourself. Let God heal the hurt that you're experiencing. Seek Him and let Him restore your heart and reveal His amazing love for you. This is where hope comes from after betrayal.

Journaling

This book talks a lot about processing your feelings. It's an important part of the healing journey to get our feelings out of our heads. To *process* your feelings simply means to think about them and honestly explore them. For most women, writing is the method of choice, though they may fight it at first. You probably won't feel like doing this step. Do it anyway—this is for you!

Get a separate notebook or diary (with a lock if privacy is an issue). Begin the process by jotting down thoughts as you read. The questions you find at the end of each chapter are simply jumping-off points. Take the truth from God's Word in the "Path Lights," and apply it directly to your situation. If you don't agree with the point or believe it, write that too. I challenge you to find the depth and breadth of God's love for you—it is limitless.

As you read, think about each emotion you are feeling. Are you feeling anger? Sadness? Disappointment? Depression? A combination? Why do you think you feel that way? At what other times in your life have you felt that way? What was the situation?

If writing is difficult for you, try cutting out images from magazines, or use rubber stamps, or draw pictures. If you're a musician, try creating music to express your feelings. Use whatever method works best to help you process your feelings. This is for you, for your eyes and ears alone, and is a critical step toward getting the most out of this book.

Journal or depict what has happened so far. Be sure to include all of your feelings. Forget everything you learned in English or art classes and simply create. It doesn't have to be pretty or spelled correctly—just process through your pen. There will be some things that your head knows are not true, but your emotions haven't caught up yet.

Write your thoughts on each truth as well as each Scripture. Think about how God's words make you feel as you read them. If they seem too good to be true, write that down as well.

Be bold and specific in your prayers to God. Tell Him what you need and then wait and see how creative He is when He answers. Go ahead and tell Him how angry you are and describe the hurt and disappointment. Be honest; He knows it all anyway. Be sure to document both your prayers and His answers.

Resources

Books About Sexual Addiction

Arterburn, Stephen, and Shannon Ethridge. *Every Heart Restored.* Colorado Springs: WaterBrook, 2004.

Cross, Clay and Rene, and Mark Tabb. *I Surrender All: Rebuilding a Marriage Broken by Pornography.* Colorado Springs: NavPress, 2005.

Means, Marsha. *Living with Your Husband's Secret Wars.* Grand Rapids: Revell, 1999.

Miller, Molly Ann. *My Husband Has a Secret: Finding Healing for the Betrayal of Sexual Addiction.* Kansas City, MO: Beacon Hill, 2005.

Roberts, Ted. *Pure Desire.* Ventura, CA: Gospel Light, 1999.

Schaumburg, Harry. *False Intimacy: Understanding the Struggle of Sexual Addiction.* Colorado Springs: NavPress, 1997.

Books About Relational Boundaries

Alcorn, Randy. *The Purity Principle: God's Safeguards for Life's Dangerous Trails.* Sisters, OR: Multnomah, 2003.

Cloud, Henry, and John Townsend. *Boundaries: When to Say Yes,*

When to Say No, to Take Control of Your Life. Grand Rapids: Zondervan, 1992.

———. *Boundaries in Marriage.* Grand Rapids: Zondervan, 1999.

———. *Safe People.* Grand Rapids: Zondervan, 1995.

Books for Personal Healing

Arterburn, Stephen, and Shannon Ethridge. *Every Woman's Battle: Discovering God's Plan for Sexual and Emotional Fulfillment.* Colorado Springs: WaterBrook, 2003.

Curtis, Brent, and John Eldredge. *The Sacred Romance: Drawing Closer to the Heart of God.* Nashville: Thomas Nelson, 1997.

Groom, Nancy. *From Bondage to Bonding: Escaping Codependence, Embracing Biblical Love.* Colorado Springs: NavPress, 1991.

Newman, Deborah. *Then God Created Woman: Finding Fulfillment as the Woman God Intended You to Be.* Colorado Springs: Focus on the Family, 1998.

Books on Marriage

Thomas, Gary. *Sacred Marriage: What If God Designed Marriage to Make Us Holy More Than to Make Us Happy?* Grand Rapids: Zondervan, 2000.

Wilson, Earl and Sandy, Paul and Virginia Friesen, and Nancy and Larry Paulson. *Restoring the Fallen: A Team Approach to Caring, Confronting and Reconciling.* Downers Grove, IL: InterVarsity, 1997.

Web Sites

www.awomanshealingjourney.com

www.hopeafterbetrayal.com

www.puredesire.org/what/partner.asp (For Men Only information and group locations)

www.pureintimacy.com

www.pureonline.com/info-for-wives.cfm

www.settingcaptivesfree.com (online course for wives, click on "A United Front")
www.skyviewcounseling.com
www.tuffstuffministries.com
www.xxxchurch.com

Computer Filters/Monitoring

Family Safe Web Filtering
   www.familysafeweb.com
Integrity Online Filtering
   www.integrityonline.com
Net Nanny Shop
   www.netnanny.com